]

Hume's *An Enq.*
Understanding

Already published in 'The SCM *Briefly* Series'

Briefly:
Hume's *An Enquiry Concerning Human Understanding*

David Mills Daniel

scm press

The Author has asserted his right under the Copyright, Designs and
Patents Act, 1988, to be identified as the Author of this Work

The author and publisher acknowledge material reproduced from
David Hume, *An Enquiry Concerning Human Understanding*, ed.
T. L. Beauchamp, Oxford and New York: Oxford University Press,
1999. ISBN 0198752482. Reprinted by permission of
Oxford University Press.

British Library Cataloguing in Publication data

A catalogue record for this book is available
from the British Library

978 0 334 04124 5

First published in 2007 by SCM Press
9–17 St Alban's Place
London NI ONX

www.scm-canterburypress.co.uk

SCM Press is a division of
SCM-Canterbury Press Ltd

Typeset by Regent Typesetting, London
Printed and bound in Great Britain by
Bookmarque Ltd, Croydon, Surrey

Contents

Introduction

The SCM *Briefly* series, edited by David Mills Daniel, is designed to enable students and general readers to acquire knowledge and understanding of key texts in philosophy, philosophy of religion, theology and ethics. While the series will be especially helpful to those following university and A-level courses in philosophy, ethics and religious studies, it will in fact be of interest to anyone looking for a short guide to the ideas of a particular philosopher or theologian.

Each book in the series takes a piece of work by one philosopher and provides a summary of the original text, which adheres closely to it, and contains direct quotations from it, thus enabling the reader to follow each development in the philosopher's argument(s). Throughout the summary, there are page references to the original philosophical writing, so that the reader has ready access to the primary text. In the Introduction to each book, you will find details of the edition of the philosophical work referred to.

In *Briefly: Hume's An Enquiry Concerning Human Understanding*, we refer to David Hume, *An Enquiry Concerning Human Understanding*, ed. T. L. Beauchamp, Oxford and New York: Oxford University Press, 1999, ISBN 0198752482.

Each *Briefly* begins with an Introduction, followed by a chapter on the Context in which the work was written. Who was this writer? Why was this book written? With Some

Introduction

Issues to Consider, and some Suggestions for Further Reading, this *Briefly* aims to get anyone started in their philosophical investigation. The Detailed Summary of the philosophical work is followed by a concise chapter-by-chapter Overview and an extensive Glossary of terms.

Bold type is used in the Detailed Summary and Overview sections to indicate the first occurrence of words and phrases that appear in the Glossary. The Glossary also contains terms used elsewhere in this *Briefly* guide and other terms that readers may encounter in their study of Hume's *An Enquiry Concerning Human Understanding*.

Context

Who was David Hume?

David Hume, perhaps the greatest British philosopher, was born in Edinburgh in 1711, and educated at Edinburgh University. He showed an early interest in philosophy, and, after living in France for a time, published his major philosophical work, the *Treatise of Human Nature* (1738–40). It was not particularly well received, but Hume's empirical approach to philosophy meant he became known as a sceptic and even an atheist. This made him an object of suspicion to the religious and cultural leaders of eighteenth-century Scotland, and may have been a factor in his not being appointed professor of philosophy at Edinburgh University in 1745. Although Hume published further works of philosophy, including *An Enquiry Concerning Human Understanding* (1748) and *An Enquiry Concerning the Principles of Morals* (1751), he turned increasingly to writing about the history of England, which brought him considerable fame. After a period as librarian to the Faculty of Advocates in Edinburgh, Hume was secretary to the British Embassy in Paris, subsequently returning to Scotland, where he died in 1776. In his autobiography, Hume described himself as cheerful, sociable and even-tempered.

What is *An Enquiry Concerning Human Understanding*?

The *Treatise of Human Nature* did not attract much interest, at least, in part, because of the inaccessible style in which it was written. Therefore, Hume decided to set out the philosophical ideas it contained in a more readable form; the two *Enquiries* were the result. In the first, *An Enquiry Concerning Human Understanding* (originally published as *Philosophical Essays Concerning Human Understanding*), Hume addresses questions of epistemology (the theory of knowledge): What do we know? How do we know what we know? What are the limits of human knowledge? On what basis do we claim to have knowledge? Does knowledge involve certainty? Does knowledge come from reason or experience? As an empiricist, Hume maintains that knowledge comes from experience; that there are definite limits to what human beings can know and that there are some questions they will never be able to answer; and that a measure of scepticism is a valuable aid to philosophical enquiry. His approach and conclusions are, therefore, very different from those of the rationalist philosopher, René Descartes who, in his *Meditations*, uses his reason to search for something absolutely certain, which will provide a secure basis for knowledge.

Hume points out (Section 1) that there are two types of philosophy: 'easy' philosophy, which is just moralizing and pointing out ways to improve human conduct; and the difficult or 'abstruse' kind, which tackles metaphysical issues. Not surprisingly, most people prefer the former, which relates to ordinary life, and find the latter unsettling. However, serious philosophical enquiry (Hume argues) is important: even society's everyday occupations and activities benefit from the spirit of accuracy that it fosters, while it is only through asking difficult philosophical questions that human beings can establish the boundaries of human knowledge, and come to accept that there some questions they cannot answer. In particular, the powers of the human understanding need to be investigated, to see how the human mind works and to discover its limits.

So where, according to Hume, does knowledge come from? He identifies (Section 2) two classes of 'mental perceptions': our immediate impressions or sensations, such as seeing and feeling, on the one hand; and our thoughts or ideas, on the other. The latter come from the former, so everything we know is based on impressions or sensations. Although this may not seem to be the case, because we have ideas (Hume gives the example of a virtuous horse), to which no impressions correspond, we are deceived by our imagination's ability to create all sorts of combinations of ideas. In fact, these complex ideas can be broken down into simple ones, which have their corresponding impressions: the idea of a virtuous horse just brings together the ideas of virtue and a familiar animal. Even the idea of an infinitely wise and good God comes from thinking about our own powers, and then imagining them as unlimited. Hume warns against our being fooled by these combinations of ideas: if we find ourselves using terms that seem to lack meaning, we need to check that there are impressions on which the ideas they refer to are based. But how do we organize our thoughts or ideas, so that they are presented to the memory or imagination in an orderly fashion?

Hume's answer (Section 3) is that we are able to do so through the three principles of association – resemblance, contiguity in place or time, and cause and effect – on which our mental operations depend. He underlines the vital role they play by illustrations from different types of literature: all the events that a historian of Europe writes about, for example, have to have unity in terms of contiguity of space and period of time.

Hume (Section 4) divides all forms of human enquiry into two groups: 'relations of ideas' and matters of fact. The first group consists of the *a priori* propositions of mathematics and logic, the truth of which can be established by thought alone, and to which the law of contradiction applies: to deny that two plus two adds up to four, for example, involves a contradiction. This is not the case with matters of fact, such as whether the sun will rise tomorrow. It is not contradictory to deny that these will occur. We know about such matters through observation and experience, which show us the 'constant conjunction' of particular things. Thus, our knowledge of cause and effect does not come from our reason, while our senses can discern nothing in an object that indicates either what caused it, or what effects it will produce. Hume points out that we tend to overlook this in relation to things with which we have been familiar from birth. We may think we have always known the effect of one billiard ball hitting another, but in theory, any outcome is possible: the first ball could return in a straight line. It is only from experience that we know that the impact of the first ball transmits motion to the second. And the fact that our knowledge of cause and effect comes from observation and experience means we cannot go beyond them: as Hume puts it, no 'sensible philosopher' tries to determine the ultimate cause of any natural process.

Hume explores the implications of the fact that, as nature does not reveal the 'secrets' of how it operates to human beings, all reasoning about empirical matters is based on our experience of the relation of cause and effect. When we see similar things, we expect them to produce similar effects to those already observed. However, past experience only tells us about particular things, at particular times. We have observed that trees shed their leaves in winter, and blossom in the spring, but there is nothing contradictory in holding that the reverse will be the case next year. The proposition that a particular thing has always produced a particular effect is not the same as the proposition that it will always produce that effect, but the second is always inferred from the first, even though there is no clear intermediate step from one to the other. The step is taken, and the inference drawn, because, after long experience of something always producing a particular effect, we feel we can be certain that it always will. However, if nature were to change, all our past experience would be useless as a guide to the future.

Hume (Section 5) makes a plea for moderate scepticism, which is a useful corrective to the human tendency to make hasty judgements and indulge in idle philosophical speculation. Although, when we reason from experience, we draw inferences that are not supported by any rational argument, and do not know the ultimate reason why a particular cause always produces a particular effect, moderate scepticism will not stop us doing so, as long as human nature remains the same. This is because habit, what Hume calls 'the principle of custom', leads us to draw such inferences, and it, not reason, is our great guide in relation to the conclusions we draw from experience. Having found, for example, that flame and heat are always connected, when we see flame, custom leads us to expect heat. And, according to Hume, this is just as well, as reason is error-prone and only develops after infancy.

But, given the imagination's ability to combine ideas into a multiplicity of fictitious forms (such as a virtuous horse), how can we distinguish between ideas that correspond to reality and the fictions of the imagination? It is the feeling of belief,

5

which Hume describes as a more 'lively' and 'steady' state of mind than that accompanying the fictions of the imagination, that enables us to do so. Hume explores how the mind works, and how the principles of association unite our thoughts. When something is presented to the senses or memory, the mind is drawn to the idea of the related object, and achieves a firmer conception of it; so, when dry wood is thrown on the fire, the mind immediately thinks it will add to, not diminish, the flame. Custom and experience moves thought from cause to effect, starting with an object present to the senses, and thus making the idea of flame livelier than it could be in the imagination. There is a pre-established harmony, based on custom, between the course of nature and the succession of our ideas. When we draw inferences (Section 6), we move from past to future, and, when an event has always occurred, expect that it always will; but, where apparently exactly similar causes have been found to produce different effects, we take this into account when deciding the probability of an event.

We think (Section 7) of certain causes and effects as being necessarily connected, but, as this is not based on any impression of a necessary connection between them, what we have is just the latter following the former. This is the case both with the causal relationship between external objects and with how the human will controls mental and physical operations. Hume notes how unreflective people think (erroneously) that they understand the causes of familiar processes, such as plant growth, but when faced with extraordinary events, such as an earthquake, fall back on God or some other supernatural cause. Philosophers, however, recognize that we do not understand the causes of even familiar events, and some attribute everything that happens to the will of God. But Hume warns that this is an example of pointless speculation. Such theories take us beyond experience and the scope of the human faculties: we know nothing about God or his attributes. As we only form the idea of necessary connection through habitually observing cause and effect, saying two events are necessarily connected means only that they have become connected in our thought. Thus, it is impossible to give a satisfactory definition of a cause. On the basis of experience, it is no more than one object, followed by another, where all the objects, similar to the first, are followed by objects, similar to the second; or, one object followed by another, the appearance of which always conveys the thought of the other.

Hume addresses (Section 8) the issue of causation or determinism (the view that every event has a cause) in relation to voluntary human actions, which he believes has been bogged down in confusion and ambiguity. In practice, people accept that causal necessity applies to human actions, agreeing that human nature remains the same down the ages; that human motives operate uniformly; and that motives like ambition and avarice always produce the same actions. We draw inferences between human actions and motives, and are able to do so only because we recognize the causal connection between the two. However, people are reluctant to acknowledge this causal connection openly, fearing it will undermine belief in free will, and damage religion and morality.

Hume argues that reconciling freedom and necessity in relation to human actions is a purely verbal question. We need to accept that actions are undeniably connected with motives, and that one follows the other. Talk of human freedom, or free will, simply means individuals being free to act, or not act, according to the determination of their will, as opposed to being subject to external constraint. Thus, there is no such thing as human freedom, when it is opposed to causal necessity, not external constraint. Hume dismisses religious and moral concerns. So far from being harmful to morality, the causal connection between motives and actions is essential to it. Unless human actions result from causes within the human character, people cannot be praised, blamed, or held responsible for them. Laws are based on the effects of rewards and punishment, which encourage good, and deter evil, actions. At the same time, we accept that people cannot be held responsible for things they do under constraint.

Hume's position is known as 'soft' determinism: human freedom or free will is compatible with determinism, and human beings are free, unless they are subject to external constraint. This position is distinct from both the libertarian one, associated with Immanuel Kant, who argues (*Groundwork of the Metaphysics of Morals*) that, for human beings to be able to subject themselves to moral laws, discovered by their reason, and to be held morally responsible for their actions, the human will must be completely free; and from that of 'hard' determinists, who maintain that the causal connection between human motives and actions rules out genuine human freedom.

Hume dismisses the argument that applying causal necessity to voluntary human actions involves a chain of necessary causes, which traces human volitions back to God's will, and makes him responsible for them. If God is the cause of all human actions, it is hard to deny he is the author of sin. But this is an example of idle philosophical speculation: better to confine philosophical enquiry to investigation of 'common life' than to embark on such a 'sea of doubt, uncertainty and contradiction'. Hume also touches on the serious issue of how to reconcile God's omniscience with human freedom (if God knows everything that is going to happen, everything that happens, including human choices, seems predetermined and inevitable), and concedes that it is beyond philosophy's power to do so.

After noting (Section 9) that, like human beings, animals also learn from experience, and conclude that the same causes will produce the same results, Hume turns to the religious issues of miracles (Section 10) and what we can learn about God's existence and attributes through the use of reason (Section 11). Although Hume does not explicitly reject belief in God or Christian teaching in his writings, his approach to religion is that of the detached philosopher, who is sceptical about religious claims and concerned about the effects of superstition and the possible excesses of popular religion. At the same time, he did not wish to cause offence, and so in both Section 11 of the *Enquiry* and his *Dialogues Concerning Natural Religion* (which he withheld from publication until after his death), presents the arguments in a form that makes it difficult to identify any one position as his.

At the beginning of Section 10, Hume makes the point that, as the evidence for Christianity and Jesus' miracles is based on human testimony, it is less than that for the truth of what our own senses tell us: this is because it is no greater, and we have more reason to believe things we see for ourselves than the testimony of others. While experience shows that, in general, human testimony can be trusted, this is not always the case, and it must be tested against experience and observation, the only reliable guides in matters of fact. When witnesses claim to have seen something that is seldom observed, experience itself should make us doubt it. This is especially the case when they claim to have witnessed a miracle, which is a violation of laws of nature that have been established on the basis of uniform human experience. Thus, the fact that

9

it would breach a law of nature (and thus cause it to cease to be one) is (Hume contends) the most powerful imaginable proof against a miracle. There is also the point as to whether the occurrence of miracles would actually help those trying to prove that God exists. As Hume argues in Section 7, it indicates greater power in God that he should have been able to create a world, which, by its normal operations, fulfils his purposes, than that he should need to intervene continually (by means of miracles), to enable it to do so. Again, we may ask why, if God intervenes sometimes, and performs miracles that, for example, help some people, on some occasions, he ignores the plight of others.

Hume suggests a test, against which all testimony about miracles should be measured. It should only be believed, if its not being true is more miraculous than the miracle itself. He applies this test to the miracles described in the Bible: the falsehood of a book, produced by an ignorant people, whose view of the world is very different from the modern one, does not seem more miraculous than the miracles it relates.

Hume puts forward further arguments against miracles: they have never been attested by sufficient people of integrity to prove they were not deluded or trying to deceive; human beings are too inclined to throw aside common sense and experience where miracles are concerned; and accounts of miracles always arise in primitive societies, or have been passed down from uneducated ancestors. He also makes the point that the miracle claims of different religions count against each other: we should treat an account of a miracle in one religion as if it referred to, and expressly contradicted, those in other religions. And saying that God caused a miracle does not make it any more probable, because we have no knowledge of his attributes, apart from what we experience of his work in the order of nature. Hume concludes by observing that the greatest miracle of all is that of faith: as reason cannot convince people of the truth of Christianity, it is the miracle of faith that enables them to accept its teachings.

In Section 11, Hume covers many of the issues discussed in greater detail in the *Dialogues*. Here he does so in the form of a friend, who imagines he is the Greek philosopher, Epicurus, defending his sceptical religious views to the Athenian public. A notable feature of the speech is its eloquent defence of freedom of thought and expression: society should not suppress opinions, because they challenge accepted religious beliefs or conventional morality.

The speech focuses on the design argument: that evidence of design in nature is the main argument for God's existence. That the order of nature is evidence of God's existence and attributes has been acknowledged in Section 10; and, in the *Dialogues*, even the sceptical Philo accepts that the cause of order in the universe probably bears some remote analogy to human intelligence. However, the point that both Philo and 'Epicurus' stress is how little this tells us about God. If a cause (God) is inferred from an effect (the universe and its order), it is not legitimate to ascribe to the inferred cause any attributes beyond those sufficient to produce the effect, or to infer from the cause other effects, beyond those by which alone it is known. If God is responsible for the existence or order of the universe, we can only ascribe to him the power, intelligence and goodness that appear in it. What we cannot do is first infer God's existence from the order of the universe, then ascribe to him perfections that have no parallel in the universe we experience, and finally, on the basis of these perfections, draw all manner of inferences about the nature of the effect, the universe, in order to make it more worthy of the cause,

God. Like Philo, 'Epicurus' is dismissive of the whole project. Those who infer an intelligent cause from the order of nature, embrace a useless idea, because, as human understanding is limited to experience, they cannot go beyond their inference.

Hume considers a possible challenge. If we saw a half-finished building, we might infer from it both that it had a designer, and that the designer would complete his work. Similarly, the universe can be thought of as an unfinished building, from which the existence of a supreme being can be inferred, and the further inference drawn that he will not leave the universe incomplete, allowing the idea of a more finished and better world to be formed. But the problem is the inadequacy of any analogy between a human artefact and the universe. With the former, we are entitled to move from effect to cause, and to form new inferences about the effect, because of our extensive experience of human beings and their artefacts. However, there is only one God and one universe, so we are not entitled to draw any further inferences.

In Section 12, Hume considers the nature of scepticism. Descartes had advocated universal doubt, in order to find an absolutely certain basis for knowledge. He thought he had found such a basis (as God does not deceive, and has inclined us to believe that what we experience comes from external objects, it must do so), but, in fact, no such secure basis exists. Thus, if Cartesian doubt had been attainable, it would have been incurable, because reason cannot establish that mental perceptions are caused by external objects, which differ from, but resemble them, rather than being created by the mind itself, or (as Descartes had imagined) being caused by an evil demon. Experience cannot decide the matter, because only the perceptions are present to the mind, and their connection with objects cannot be experienced.

This seems to be a triumph for the sceptics, but (Hume contends) scepticism, instead of providing answers, just creates hesitation and doubt. Scepticism about matters of fact is either popular or philosophical. The first, arising from limitations of human understanding, and people having different opinions about things, is weak, and everyday activity is the best way to dispose of it: sceptical views may flourish in the study, but quickly vanish in the outside world, where they are impossible to sustain.

Philosophical scepticism is more difficult to dismiss, as it can be argued that, apart from sense and memory, the relation of cause and effect is our only evidence for any matter of fact; that this derives from observing the constant conjunction of objects; and that we have no basis, apart from custom or instinct, for believing that this will continue. The most powerful objection to this form of scepticism is that it does no good. People would sink into total inactivity, if they lived by such views. But nature is too strong, and even the most extreme sceptic does not lead his life as if he actually believes what he professes. He will live as others do: acting, reasoning and believing, even though they cannot satisfy themselves about the basis of their beliefs.

However (Hume maintains), while extreme scepticism is valueless and unsustainable, limited scepticism highlights the limitations of human understanding, curbs dogmatism, and makes people more receptive to the views of others. It helps convince us to confine our enquiries to subjects, suited to the narrow limits of human understanding. There are many things in ordinary life and experience we cannot explain, and so we should concentrate on these, and accept that we are unlikely to reach satisfactory conclusions about such matters as the origin of the universe. Hume concludes with a famous passage, in which he suggests that, as experience is the source of human knowledge, we should commit books about divinity or metaphysics, which try to go beyond it, to the flames as sophistry and illusion.

Is the theory of knowledge that Hume sets out in the first *Enquiry* convincing? For the empiricist, experience is the only or main source of knowledge, but is this the case, or does reason also play a major part? It is not just (as Hume notes in Section 12) that we need reason to correct the evidence of the senses, as when an oar looks crooked in water; there is also the question of the origin of the general categories of thought, such as space, time, substance and causation, which enable us to organize the information we receive through the senses. Do these also come from experience? We may prefer to agree with Kant (*Critique of Pure Reason*), that although knowledge begins with experience, it does not all come from experience:

> That all our knowledge begins with experience there can be no doubt. For how is it possible that the faculty of knowledge should be awakened into exercise otherwise than by means of objects which affect our senses . . . But, though all our knowledge begins with experience, it by no means follows, that all arises out of experience . . . on the contrary, it is quite possible that our empirical knowledge is a compound of that which we receive through impressions, and that which the faculty of knowledge supplies from itself.

However, Hume's first *Enquiry* is a bold and highly readable statement of the empiricist case, which also provides thought-provoking and controversial discussion of a range of philosophical issues, from determinism and free will to the possibility of miracles.

Some Issues to Consider

- In *An Enquiry Concerning Human Understanding,* David Hume addresses questions of epistemology: what we know; how we know what we know; and whether our knowledge comes from reason or experience.
- Hume maintains that society benefits from the spirit of accuracy that philosophical investigation fosters, while asking difficult philosophical questions marks out the limits of human knowledge, and shows that there are some questions human beings will never be able to answer.
- Hume divides mental perceptions into immediate impressions or sensations, such as seeing and feeling, and thoughts or ideas; the latter come from the former, so everything we know is based on impressions or sensations.
- Complex ideas can be broken down into simple ones, which have their corresponding impressions, and Hume warns us not to be fooled by the fact that our imaginations can create all sorts of combinations of ideas: if we find ourselves using terms that seem to lack meaning, we need to check there are impressions on which the ideas they refer to are based.
- Is Hume right to hold that we organize our thoughts through three principles of association: resemblance, contiguity in place or time, and cause and effect, and that our mental operations depend on them?
- Hume divides all forms of human enquiry into two groups: relations of ideas, the truth of which can be established by thought alone; and matters of fact, which we know about through observation and experience.
- According to Hume, our knowledge of cause and effect does not come from our reason, but from experience, which shows us that certain things always follow each other.

Context

- When we see similar things, we expect them to produce similar effects to those already observed, but Hume points out that the proposition that a particular thing has always produced the same effect is not the same as the proposition that it always will.

- Is Hume right to maintain that, although we do not know why a particular cause produces a particular effect, habit or custom leads us to infer that it will continue to do so?

- Hume thinks that belief, the steady and lively state of mind that accompanies ideas that correspond to reality, enables us to distinguish these from the fictions of the imagination.

- According to Hume, when human beings try to determine the probability of an event, they move from past to future, and take into account whether or not apparently similar causes have been found to produce the same or different effects.

- Hume argues that the idea of the necessary connection of certain causes and effects comes from our habitually observing one thing following another.

- This means that it is not possible to give a better definition of a cause than one thing followed by another, where all the things, similar to the first, are followed by things similar to the second, or one thing followed by another, the appearance of which always conveys the thought of the other.

- Is it true, as Hume contends, that causal necessity applies to human actions, and that there is no such thing as free will, when it is opposed to causal necessity, not external constraint?

- Is he also right to believe that a causal connection between human motives and actions is consistent with people being held morally responsible for their actions?

- Hume believes that the fact that it would breach a law of nature, which has been established on the basis if uniform human experience, is the most powerful imaginable proof against a miracle.

- Hume lays down a test for reports of miracles: they should only be believed, if their not being true is more miraculous than the miracle itself; and argues that the miracle claims of one religion should be treated as contradicting those of other religions.

- Does evidence of design in nature enable us to prove God's existence, and tell us something about his attributes?

- Hume points out that, even if God is responsible for the existence or order of the universe, we can only ascribe to him the power, intelligence and goodness that appear in it.

- Is it legitimate to draw an analogy between the universe and a half-finished building, or does the analogy break down for the reasons Hume gives?

- For Hume, there can be no absolutely certain basis for knowledge, and he thinks that, if Cartesian doubt were attainable, it would be incurable.

- This is because neither reason nor experience can establish that mental perceptions are caused by external objects, which differ from, but resemble them, rather than being created by the mind itself, or (as Descartes had imagined) being caused by an evil demon: experience cannot decide the matter, because only perceptions are present to the mind, and their connection with objects cannot be experienced.

- But this does not mean that extreme scepticism should be allowed to triumph: in Hume's view, the main objections to extreme scepticism are that it does no good, and is unsustainable.

- Do you agree with Hume that limited scepticism is valuable as a means of highlighting the limitations of human understanding, curbing dogmatism and making people more receptive to the views of others?

Suggestions for Further Reading

David Hume, *Dialogues Concerning Natural Religion*, ed. R. H. Popkin, second edition, Indianapolis/Cambridge: Hackett Publishing Company, 1998.

David Hume, *A Natural History of Religion*, ed. H. E. Root, Stanford: Stanford University Press, 1957.

David Hume, *A Treatise of Human Nature*, ed. E. C. Mossner, London: Penguin, 1969.

David Hume, *An Enquiry Concerning Human Understanding*, ed. T. L. Beauchamp, Oxford and New York: Oxford University Press, 1999.

David Hume, *An Enquiry Concerning the Principles of Morals*, ed. J. B. Stewart, second edition, Illinois: Open Court Publishing, 1966.

A. J. Ayer, *Hume: A Very Short Introduction*, Oxford and New York: Oxford University Press, 2000.

A. J. Ayer, *Language, Truth and Logic*, reprinted with an Introduction by Ben Rogers, London: Penguin Books, 2001.

V. C. Chappell (ed.), *Hume*, London: Macmillan, 1968.

F. Copleston, *A History of Philosophy*, Vol. 5, Part II (Berkeley to Hume), New York NY: Image Books, 1964.

R. Descartes, *Discourse on Method and Meditations on First Philosophy*, trans. D. A. Cress, fourth edition, Indianapolis/Cambridge: Hackett Publishing Company, 1998.

J. C. A. Gaskin, 1988, *Hume's Philosophy of Religion*, second edition, London: Macmillan.

I. Kant, *Critique of Pure Reason*, ed. V. Politis, London: Everyman, 1997.

I. Kant, *Groundwork of the Metaphysics of Morals*, ed. M. Gregor, Cambridge: Cambridge University Press, 1997.

J. E. C. Mossner, *The Life of David Hume*, second edition, Oxford and New York: Oxford University Press, 1980.

J. L. Mackie, *The Cement of the Universe*, Oxford: Clarendon Press, 1974.

D. F. Norton (ed.), *The Cambridge Companion to Hume*, Cambridge: Cambridge University Press, 1993.

J. Passmore, *Hume's Intentions*, revised edition, London: Duckworth, 1968.

R. Swinburne, *The Existence of God*, revised edition, Oxford: Clarendon Press, 1991.

P. Vardy, *The Puzzle of God*, revised edition, London: Fount Paperbacks, 1999.

Detailed Summary of Hume's *An Enquiry Concerning Human Understanding*

Section 1
Of the Different Species of Philosophy (pp. 87–95)

There are two ways of treating '**Moral philosophy**, or the **science of human nature**' (p. 87). One type of **philosopher** treats human beings as 'chiefly as born for action', and, as '**virtue**' is held to be the 'most valuable' object, discusses it in ways designed to 'please the **imagination**', in order to direct our 'steps in these paths by the soundest **precepts** and most illustrious examples' (p. 87). They make us feel the difference between 'vice and virtue', in order to persuade us to 'love of **probity**' (p. 87). The other type sees human beings as primarily 'reasonable', and wants to develop our 'understanding' (p. 87). They investigate the 'principles' that 'regulate' our understanding, and lead us to 'approve or blame' actions or objects; and think it is a weakness that **philosophy** has not yet established the 'foundation of morals, reasoning and criticism' (p. 87). Their approach moves from 'particular instances to general principles', until they reach the 'original principles', and, thereby, the limits of what can be known (p. 88). They hope to discover 'hidden truths', which may instruct 'posterity' (p. 88). For the most part, the 'generality of mankind' prefers '**easy**' **philosophy** of the first type: it relates more closely to 'common life', and helps to reform 'conduct', while '**abstruse philosophy**' has limited 'influence over our conduct' (p. 88). A 'profound philosopher' may make an error, which leads to further ones, until his 'subtle reasonings' completely contradict 'popular opinion' (p. 88). On the other hand, a philosopher, who depends upon an 'appeal to common sense', is more likely to get back on to 'the right path', and be esteemed by future generations (p. 88). Thus, today, '**CICERO**' is more highly regarded than '**ARISTOTLE**', while '**ADDISON**' is widely read, but '**LOCKE**' will probably be 'forgotten' (pp. 88–9). Indeed, the 'mere philosopher' is thought to contribute little benefit to 'society': although sheer ignorance is 'still more despised' (p. 89). The 'perfect character' is thought to lie between the two 'extremes': an individual, who is equally comfortable with 'books, company, and business', and who conducts his life by 'noble sentiments and wise precepts', which apply to every '**exigence of human life**' (p. 89).

Human beings are intellectual, 'sociable' and 'active' beings, so their 'nature' indicates that a 'mixed' life suits them best (p. 89). They should pursue knowledge in a way that relates it to 'action and society' (p. 89). Excessive preoccupation with 'abstruse thought' results in 'uncertainty' and 'melancholy', while its 'discoveries' are often given a 'cold reception' by others (pp. 89–90). Now, if it were just a matter of people preferring 'easy philosophy', it might be right to let the matter pass (p. 90). However, they seem to reject any 'profound reasonings', such as '*metaphysics*' (p. 90). So, is there anything to be said in its defence?

'Accurate and **abstract philosophy**' does serve the needs of society (p. 90). Even those who wish to write about, or paint, the 'outward appearances of life and manners' do so more successfully, if they have knowledge of 'the understanding, the workings of the passions', and of the feelings that discriminate between 'vice and virtue' (p. 90). The anatomist's work may seem disagreeable, but is instructive for those wishing to paint 'a **VENUS** or an **HELEN**', who need to know the 'inward structure of the human body' (p. 90). Whatever people do, they benefit from a 'spirit of accuracy', and, even though philosophers may keep aloof from society, the 'genius of philosophy' will 'gradually' permeate society, endowing 'every art and calling' with its accurate approach (pp. 90–1). Furthermore, the 'sweetest' path in life 'leads through the avenues of science and learning', and, although research may be 'painful and fatiguing', there are minds that thrive on the 'severe exercise', while bringing 'light from obscurity' is always 'delightful' (p. 91).

But it is said that 'abstract philosophy', as well as being 'painful and fatiguing', also causes 'uncertainty and error', and that much metaphysics results either from human beings trying to grasp what is 'inaccessible to the understanding', or from '**popular superstitions**' (p. 91). However, is not this a reason for philosophers to persist in their efforts? The only way of 'freeing learning' from these 'abstruse questions' is to investigate 'the nature of human understanding', and to show, by 'exact analysis of its powers and capacity', that it is unsuited to such 'subjects' (p. 92). Only 'accurate and just reasoning' will enable us to cut through 'abstruse philosophy and **metaphysical jargon**' (p. 92).

Further, 'accurate scrutiny' of human 'powers and faculties' is important (p. 92). Whenever we reflect on the 'operations of the mind', they seem 'involved in obscurity' (p. 92). We need to distinguish them from each other, put them in order, and 'class them under their proper heads' (p. 92). Ignorance of human '**mental geography**' should be considered 'contempt-ible' in those who profess to love 'learning and philosophy' (p. 93). Such an investigation is within our capabilities. We perceive that the mind has several distinct 'powers and fac-ulties', such as 'the **will**', 'understanding', 'imaginatìon' and 'passions', and that these can be more precisely 'distinguished by reflection' (p. 93). Indeed, it is not unreasonable to hope that philosophy could, in some degree, discover the 'secret springs', by which 'the human mind is actuated in its oper-ations', just as **that 'philosopher'** did the 'laws and forces, by which the **revolutions of the planets** are governed' (p. 93). It is likely that one mental 'operation and principle' depends on another, which may then be 'resolved' into another 'more gen-eral and universal' one (pp. 93–4). We must not be pessimistic about the prospects of success: indeed, such a 'conclusion' is not 'desirable' (p. 94). '**Moralists**', viewing the range of differ-ent actions that 'excite our approbation or dislike', have sought a 'general principle' to explain the 'variety' of our '**sentiments**'; and their efforts have not been 'wholly unsuccessful' (p. 94). To abandon them would be 'rash' and 'dogmatical' (p. 94). The research may be hard and painful, but we will gain both 'profit' and 'pleasure', if, through them, we can increase our 'knowledge' of such important 'subjects' (p. 94).

This enquiry tries to throw light on matters, from which 'uncertainty' has 'deterred the wise, and obscurity the ignor-ant' (pp. 94–5). We shall rejoice if we can unite 'profound en-quiry with clearness, and truth with novelty', and 'undermine the foundations of an abstruse philosophy' that has been a 'shelter to superstition' (p. 95).

Section 2
Of the Origin of Ideas (pp. 96–100)

All will acknowledge the difference between '**perceptions of the mind**', as, for example, when someone 'feels the pain of excessive heat', and remembering or imagining such a '**sensation**', which lacks the 'force and vivacity' of the 'original' (p. 96). Not even the most 'splendid' poetry can depict 'natural objects' in such a way that the 'description' is 'taken for a real landscape': the 'most lively thought is still inferior to the dullest sensation' (p. 96). A similar distinction applies to 'other perceptions': actual anger is very different from thinking of it (p. 96). Thought is a 'faithful mirror' of 'past sentiments and affections', but is 'faint and dull' beside the 'original perceptions' (p. 96). Thus, we can divide mental 'perceptions' into 'two classes', the less vivid 'THOUGHTS OR **IDEAS**', and what we might call '**IMPRESSIONS**', the 'more lively perceptions' of, for example, hearing, seeing, feeling and so on (pp. 96–7).

Human thought seems at first 'unbounded', even by 'the limits of nature and reality' (p. 97). The body may be 'confined to one planet', but thought can take us to the universe's 'most distant regions' (p. 97). It can conceive things that have never been 'seen, or heard' (p. 97). Nothing is beyond its 'power', except 'what implies an **absolute contradiction**' (p. 97). However, on reflection, its limits are found to be 'very narrow' (p. 97). This 'creative power' is only the '**faculty of compounding, transposing, augmenting**' the information provided by 'the **senses** and **experience**' (p. 97). If we think of a 'virtuous horse', we unite virtue with a 'familiar' animal: so, 'all our ideas or more feeble perceptions are copies of our impressions or more lively ones' (p. 97). Even our most '**sublime**' ideas can be analysed into 'simple' ones (p. 97). The 'idea of God', as '*an* *infinitely intelligent, wise, and good Being*', derives from reflection on our own mental 'operations', and 'augmenting, without limit' our own 'qualities of goodness and wisdom' (pp. 97–8). Those, who disagree with 'this position', must refute it by producing an idea 'not derived from this source' (p. 98).

If a 'defect' makes someone incapable of a particular kind of sensation, he will not possess 'the **correspondent ideas**' (p. 98). Thus, a blind person can 'form no notion of colours' (p. 98). In 'a less degree', the same is true of the **passions** (p. 98). A mild-tempered person has no idea of '**inveterate** revenge or cruelty', nor does a selfish one 'easily' have an idea of 'generosity' (p. 98). There is one '**contradictory phaenomenon**' (p. 98). Colours differ from, but at the same time resemble each other, as do the 'different shades of the same colour' (p. 98). If someone, who had become blind as an adult, knew all the colours, apart from a 'particular shade of blue', is it not possible that he might 'raise up' that shade from his imagination, although he had never seen it (pp. 98–9)? This suggests that '**simple ideas**' are not always derived from the 'correspondent impressions', but the case is a 'singular' one, and does not justify altering 'our general **maxim**' (p. 99).

This 'proposition' could dispel all the 'jargon' that characterizes 'metaphysical reasonings' (p. 99). All ideas, particularly 'abstract ones', are 'faint and obscure', and liable to be confused with others that resemble them; and, when we use a term frequently, even if it has no 'distinct meaning', we tend to think it has 'a **determinate** idea, annexed to it' (p. 99). But impressions are 'strong and vivid', and it is harder to make mistakes about them (p. 99). So, if we use a 'philosophical term', which lacks 'any meaning or idea', we must ask '*from what impression is that supposed idea derived?*' (p. 99). If there seems not to be one, this will 'confirm our suspicion' (p. 99).

Bringing ideas into 'so clear a light' should help to 'remove all dispute' about 'their nature and reality' (p. 99).

Section 3
Of the Association of Ideas (pp. 101–7)

There is a **'principle of connexion'** between the mind's different 'thoughts or ideas', so they present themselves to the 'memory or imagination' with 'method and regularity' (p. 101). When we are thinking seriously, any thought that breaks into our 'chain of ideas' is 'rejected', while, even in dreams, the 'different ideas' are connected (p. 101). Even in 'different languages', it can be seen that the words which express the 'most compounded' ideas are held together by some 'universal principle', which equally influences 'all mankind' (p. 101). But, although 'different ideas' are obviously 'connected together' in this way, no philosopher has tried to classify 'all the **principles of association'** (p. 101). There seem to be three: '*Resemblance, Contiguity* in time or place and *Cause* or *Effect*' (p. 101). These 'principles' connect ideas, but it may be hard to prove that there are no other 'principles of association' (pp. 101–2). We can only look at 'instances', and examine the principle that 'binds the different thoughts', until we make it 'as general as possible' (p. 102).

In all 'compositions of genius', the writer has a 'plan or object': a piece of writing without 'a design' would be like the 'ravings of a madman' (p. 102). In 'narrative compositions', the events must be 'related to each other in the imagination', and form a 'kind of *Unity*', although the 'connecting principle' will differ, according to the writer's specific aim (p. 102). **OVID** uses 'resemblance': any manifestation of the gods' 'miraculous' powers suffices to bring it under 'his original plan' (pp. 102–3). A historian of Europe would be influenced by 'contiguity in time and place' (p. 103). However 'different and unconnected' the events he wrote about were, in this respect, they would have 'unity' (p. 103). The most common 'species of connexion' in 'narrative composition' is 'cause and effect' (p. 103). The historian's subject is some part of the 'great chain of events', of which the 'history of mankind' consists, and he tries to cover each 'link' in it (p. 103). This 'connexion' being the 'strongest of all', he is aware that knowledge of it is the 'most instructive', since it alone enables us to '**controul events, and govern futurity**' (p. 103).

This gives us some idea of the 'notion of *Unity* of *Action*', of which 'all critics, after ARISTOTLE', have talked so much (p. 103). A 'certain unity' is required in all literary 'productions' (p. 103). Both a biographer of '**ACHILLES**' and a poet, writing about his 'anger', would 'connect the events, by showing their mutual dependence and relation' (p. 103). A person's actions depend 'on each other', not only during a limited period of his life, but throughout its 'duration': removing 'one link' would affect the 'whole series of events' (pp. 103–4). In '**epic poetry**', this 'connexion' is particularly 'close and sensible': the imagination and passions of 'writer and reader' are both 'more enlivened' and 'enflamed' than in, for example, history or biography (p. 104). Why do these require a 'stricter and closer unity in the fable' (p. 104)? Poetry brings us nearer to 'the objects' it deals with than other types of 'narration', and, by throwing a strong 'light' on 'minute circumstances', gratifies 'the fancy' (p. 104). If a poet were to include a 'great compass of time or series of events', he would 'draw out his poem to an immeasurable length' (p. 104). His 'reader's imagination' and 'passions' would be so 'enflamed' by the 'repeated violence of the same movements' that they would 'flag' long before the end (p. 104). Further, the epic poet 'must not trace the causes to any great distance' (p. 104). While the central characters are involved in one 'common scene', with each action 'strongly connected with the whole', the 'passions' move easily from 'one object to another' (p. 105). However, if the poet introduces new characters, not connected with the others, the imagination will be conscious of the break, and will 'enter coldly into the new scene' (p. 105).

The same thing happens when the poet traces 'events to too great a distance', and brings together loosely related actions (p. 105). This is the reason for the 'oblique narration', used in the '*Odyssey* and *Aenid*', in which the hero is first shown close to accomplishing 'his designs', while more 'distant events and causes' are introduced later (p. 105). This immediately engages 'the reader's curiosity' (p. 105). Again, in 'dramatic poetry', the 'spectator's concern' must not be 'diverted' by scenes that are unconnected with 'the rest', as such a 'breach' disrupts the 'communication' of emotions, by which 'one scene adds force to another' (p. 105).

Going back to the 'comparison of history and epic poetry', all this indicates that, as a 'certain unity' is required in epic poetry and drama, it cannot be 'wanting in history'; and that, in the latter, what connects 'the several events', as in 'epic poetry', is 'the relation of cause and effect' (p. 106). In epic poetry, the connections will be closer, due to the extent to which the poet touches the 'imagination' and 'passions' (p. 106). Thus, while the '**PELOPONNESIAN war**' is a suitable subject for history, the '**siege of ATHENS**' is more appropriate for an 'epic poem' (p. 106). However, as we are talking about different 'degrees of connexion', the exact 'bounds' that separate the two are hard to 'determine' (p. 106).

Homer, in his treatment of 'ACHILLES' and '**HECTOR**',

manages to 'produce a sufficient unity in the subject', as does **Milton**, in *Paradise Lost*, although he does trace 'his causes to too great a distance' (p. 106). The 'loose hints', set out above, indicate that many of the human mind's 'operations' depend on the 'connexion or association of ideas' (p. 107). The 'sympathy' between the 'passions and imagination' is particularly noteworthy, and it can be seen that 'the affections' that one object arouses pass 'easily' into another, 'connected with it', but not into unconnected ones (p. 107). Thorough investigation of 'this principle' would result in 'reasonings too profound and too copious for this enquiry': it is enough to have established that 'the three connecting principles of all ideas are the relations of *Resemblance, Contiguity*, and **Causation**' (p. 107).

Section 4
Sceptical Doubts Concerning the Operations of the Understanding (pp. 108–18)

Part 1 (pp. 108–13)

All 'objects of human reason or enquiry' divide into 'two kinds': '*Relations of Ideas* and *Matters of Fact*' (p. 108). The first includes every 'affirmation' that is '**demonstratively certain**', such as those of geometry and arithmetic: for example, '*three times five is equal to the half of thirty*' (p. 108). The truth of such propositions is discovered by the 'mere operation of thought', and does not depend on what exists 'in the **universe**' (p. 108). 'Matters of fact' are very different, because their 'contrary' never implies a 'contradiction' (p. 108). So, for example, the proposition, '*the sun will not rise to-morrow*' is 'intelligible', and its 'falsehood' cannot be demonstrated (p. 108). So, what evidence 'assures us' of a 'matter of fact' beyond the 'testimony of our senses' and 'our memory' (p. 108)? This 'part of philosophy' has been neglected by both ancient and modern philosophers (pp. 108–9).

Reasoning about matters of fact seems to be based on the 'relation of *Cause* and *Effect*', which enables us to 'go beyond the evidence of our memory and senses' (p. 109). Thus, someone finding 'a watch' on a 'desert island' would conclude there had 'once been men' there (p. 109). If we analyse other 'reasonings of this nature', we shall find them to be based on 'the relation of cause and effect', which is either 'near or remote, or direct or **collateral**' (p. 109). Heat and light are 'collateral effects of fire': one may 'justly be inferred from the other' (p. 109). How do we 'arrive at the knowledge of cause and effect' (p. 109)? It is not obtained by 'reasonings *a priori*', but is the result of the 'experience' of finding that 'particular objects are constantly conjoined with each other' (p. 109). No object discloses, through the 'qualities which appear to the senses', either the 'causes' that 'produced it', or the 'effects' that will 'arise from it': 'reason, unassisted by experience', cannot 'draw any inference concerning real existence and matter of fact' (p. 110). We can confirm that causes and effects are '*discoverable*' only through '*experience*' by remembering that, before we became familiar with particular objects, we had no way of 'foretelling what would arise from them' (p. 110). For example, 'the explosion of gunpowder, or the attraction of a **loadstone**' could not be 'discovered by arguments *a priori*' (p. 110). However, we may not think this applies to events that have 'become familiar to us from our first appearance in the world' (p. 110). We tend to think that we could infer immediately that 'one billiard ball would communicate motion to another upon impulse' (p. 110). This shows how great the 'influence of custom' is (p. 110).

If we were asked to say what the 'effect' of a particular object would be, without 'consulting past **observation**', how could we do it (p. 111)? As the effect cannot be found in the 'supposed cause', we would have to 'invent or imagine' it, which would be 'entirely arbitrary' (p. 111). For example, 'motion in the second billiard ball' is 'quite distinct' from that in the first, so without 'experience', we might think that any effect could 'result from the operation of that cause' (p. 111). I might imagine a 'hundred different events' following one billiard ball striking another, such as the first ball returning 'in a straight line': and 'reasonings *a priori*' cannot tell us which is correct (p. 111). Attempting to 'determine any single event, or infer any cause or effect', without using 'observation and experience', would be 'vain' (p. 111).

This is why no 'rational and modest' philosopher has tried to 'assign the **ultimate cause of any natural operation**' (pp. 111–12). The most human beings can do is to 'resolve the many particular effects into a few general causes', by reasoning from 'analogy, experience, and observation' (p. 112). But we will never discover the 'causes of these general causes': these 'ultimate springs and principles' are proof against 'human curiosity' (p. 112). The best we can hope to do is (as far as possible) trace 'particular phaenomena' back to 'these general principles' (p. 112). It may be that the 'most perfect philosophy' serves only to emphasize 'our ignorance' and highlight our 'blindness and weakness' (p. 112). Geometry, when invoked in aid of '**natural philosophy**', does not, despite its 'accuracy of reasoning', yield 'knowledge of ultimate causes' (p. 112). Such '**mixed mathematics**' is based on the assumption that there are 'certain laws', such as the '**law of motion**', which are 'established by nature' (p. 112). Geometry helps in the 'application' of such laws, but 'discovery of the law' is due to 'experience'

(p. 112). 'Abstract reasonings' about an object could not suggest the 'effect' it will cause, or indicate the 'inseparable and inviolable connexion' between cause and effect (pp. 112–13). It would require a 'very sagacious' person to discover 'by reasoning' that 'crystal is the effect of heat' (p. 113).

Part 2 (pp. 113–18)

Our *'reasonings concerning matter of fact'* seem to be based on 'the relation of cause and effect', while our conclusions *'concerning that relation'* seem to be drawn from 'EXPERIENCE' (p. 113). But what is the *'foundation of all conclusions from experience'* (p. 113)? I can only 'give a negative answer': they are *'not* founded on reasoning, or any process of the understanding' (p. 113). The fact is that 'nature' keeps us 'at a great distance from all her secrets' (p. 113). For example, 'our senses' tell us the 'colour, weight, and consistence' of bread, but neither 'sense nor reason' can tell us how it nourishes the 'human body' (p. 113). It is accepted that the mind does not reach conclusions on the basis of anything it knows about the 'nature' of such objects (p. 114). However, though ignorant of 'natural powers and principles', we take it that, when we see 'like sensible qualities', they have 'like secret powers', and expect that 'effects, similar to those' we have experienced, will 'follow from them' (p. 114).

'Past *Experience*' does give us *'direct* and *certain* information' about particular objects at a particular 'period of time', but why do we extend this experience 'to future times' and 'other objects' (p. 114)? An 'inference' is made, which needs 'to be explained' (p. 114). The following 'propositions' are not 'the same': *'I have found that such an object has always been attended with such an* effect', so *'I foresee'* that other objects, similar *'in appearance'*, will be *'attended with similar effects'* (p. 114). Now, the second proposition is 'always' inferred from the first, but, as the 'connexion' between them is not 'intuitive', by what 'chain of reasoning' (p. 114)? What is the 'connecting proposition' or 'intermediate step' (p. 115)?

Reasoning can be 'divided into two kinds': **demonstrative reasoning**, concerning **'relations of ideas'**, and **reasoning 'concerning matter of fact and existence'** (p. 115). The first kind does not apply in this 'case', as there is no 'contradiction' involved in holding that an object, similar to those we have experienced, may produce 'different or contrary effects' (p. 115). It is not contradictory 'to affirm', for example, that the trees will 'flourish' in January, and 'decay' in May (p. 115). Thus, we are concerned with the second group, but the argument that we should trust 'past experience' can be 'probable only' (p. 115). Our arguments, relating to existence and matters of fact, are based on 'cause and effect'; our knowledge of that derives 'from experience'; and all 'experimental conclusions' presuppose that 'the future' will conform to 'the past' (p. 115). So, we find ourselves 'going in a circle' (p. 115).

All 'arguments from experience' are grounded on the 'similarity, which we discover among natural objects': from causes that 'appear *similar*, we expect similar effects', and this is the 'sum of all our experimental conclusions' (p. 116). Now, if it were 'formed by reason', this conclusion, though based on 'one instance', would be 'perfect' (p. 116). However, it is only after a 'long course of uniform experiments' that we reach 'firm reliance and security' about a 'particular event' (p. 116).

So, what is the 'process of reasoning', by which we draw a different conclusion from 'one instance' than from 'a hundred', which in no way differs from the first (p. 116)? It could be said that we *'infer* a connexion between the sensible qualities and the secret powers', but this does not answer the question as to the 'process of argument', on which the inference is based (p. 116). How does experience, merely by showing us 'a number of uniform effects' from 'certain objects', remedy our 'ignorance' of the 'powers and influence of all objects' (p. 116)? We expect similar effects from similar objects, but this is a 'step or progress of the mind', which needs explaining (p. 117). It is not **'intuitive'** or 'demonstrative', and it begs the question to call it 'experimental', as all 'inferences from experience' suppose that 'the future will resemble the past' (p. 117). As experience would be 'useless', if 'nature' changed, and the past ceased to be a 'rule for the future', 'arguments from experience' cannot prove the 'resemblance' of past to future, as they are based on it (p. 117). However 'regular' things are, this does not prove they will be so in 'the future', so, as 'a philosopher', I want to know what stops us thinking they will 'not happen always' (p. 117)? Even the most 'stupid peasants', 'infants' and animals 'improve by experience', and learn about natural objects from 'observing the effects' (p. 118). It cannot be said that they do so 'by any process of argument or **ratiocination**' (p. 118). The 'proposition' I wish to 'enforce' here is that it is not 'reasoning' that leads us to expect the past to resemble the future, or apparently similar 'causes' to produce 'similar effects' (p. 118).

Section 5
Sceptical Solution of these Doubts (pp. 119–30)

Part 1 (pp. 119–24)

Although it aims at 'extirpation of our vices', the 'passion for philosophy' can result in our reasoning ourselves out of 'all virtue': by focusing on the 'vanity of human life', we may just be looking for reasons to indulge 'natural indolence' (p. 119). But this does not apply to 'ACADEMIC or SCEPTICAL philosophy', whose followers always urge the need to avoid 'hasty' judgements, and philosophical 'speculations' outside the 'limits of common life' (p. 119). This 'philosophy' curbs 'indolence of the mind', while preventing 'lofty pretensions' and 'superstitious credulity' (p. 119). Thus, it is surprising that it receives so much criticism: but, perhaps it is its very opposition to so many 'vices and follies' that creates 'enemies' (pp. 119–20).

We need not be afraid that this kind of moderate scepticism will 'undermine the reasonings of common life', or raise doubts that will 'destroy all action' (p. 120). We may conclude (as in the 'foregoing section') that, in reasoning from experience, the mind takes 'a step', which is 'not supported by any argument'; but there is 'no danger' that 'these reasonings', on which 'all knowledge depends', will be 'affected' (p. 120). While human nature 'remains the same', whatever 'principle' leads us to 'make this step' will 'preserve its influence' (p. 120). An intelligent newcomer to 'this world' would 'observe a continual succession of objects', but would not, 'at first', discover 'the idea of cause and effect', as it is not 'reasonable' to suppose that, just because one event 'precedes' another, it is its 'cause' (p. 120). Without 'more experience', such a person would be unable to reason about 'any matter of fact' that was not 'immediately present to his memory and senses' (p. 120). However, after a while, through observing the constant conjunction of certain 'objects or events', he will infer the 'existence of one' from the 'appearance of the other', even though he still does not know how one 'produces the other' (pp. 120–1).

What leads him to do so is the **'principle' of 'CUSTOM or HABIT'** (p. 121). When we use this term, we acknowledge that we do not know the 'ultimate reason' why 'a particular act or operation' is repeated: 'our faculties' can take us 'no farther' in discovering it (p. 121). Custom is the 'ultimate principle' of 'human nature', in relation to 'all our conclusions from experience'; it is the only 'hypothesis' that explains why we draw from 'a thousand instances' of, for example, the 'constant conjunction' of 'heat and flame', an inference that we are unable to draw from just one, which in no way differs from them (p. 120). Thus, 'all inferences from experience' are 'effects of custom', which is the 'great guide of human life', not 'reasoning' (pp. 121–2). Without it, we would know nothing 'beyond what is immediately present to the memory and senses', and would be unable to use 'our natural powers' to produce 'any effect' (pp. 122–3).

However, although our 'conclusions from experience' take us beyond 'memory and senses', 'some fact' must be 'present to the senses or memory', to lead us to draw them (p. 123). If we did not start with some immediately 'present' fact, our 'reasonings' would be 'hypothetical'; the 'whole chain of inferences' would be unsupported; and we would not achieve 'knowledge of any real existence' (p. 123). What all this leads to is the 'simple' conclusion that: 'all belief of matter of fact or real existence is derived merely from some object', which is 'present to the memory or senses', and 'a customary conjunction' between it and 'some other object' (p. 123). Once we have found, for example, that 'flame and heat' are always 'conjoined together', if flame is 'presented anew to the senses', custom leads the mind to expect heat, and to '*believe*' that 'such a quality' exists (p. 123). We are talking here of 'a species of natural instincts', which no 'process of the thought' can produce or prevent (pp. 123–4). We could stop our 'philosophical researches' here, as, in 'most questions', we can advance no further (p. 124). But it is understandable that we wish to examine more closely the 'nature of this *belief*', and the '*customary conjunction*', from which it derives (p. 124).

Part 2 (pp. 124–30)

Although the human 'imagination' cannot 'exceed' the 'stock of ideas' it receives from the senses, it has an 'unlimited power' of 'mixing, compounding' and 'dividing' them (p. 124). So what is the difference between 'fiction and belief' (p. 124)? It is some 'sentiment or feeling', 'annexed' to the latter, which cannot be 'commanded at pleasure', but must be 'excited by nature' (p. 124). For, as there is no 'matter of fact', which we 'believe so firmly' that we 'cannot conceive the contrary', such a 'sentiment' constitutes the only 'difference' between a 'conception' we accept, and one we reject (p. 125). There is no 'contradiction' in conceiving' a 'billiard ball' stopping on 'contact' with another, but it 'feels' very different from the 'conception' of one ball communicating motion 'to another' (p. 125). This 'feeling' is '*Belief*', which is a more 'lively' and 'steady conception of an object' than the imagination can achieve, so it is 'evident' that belief is to do with how ideas are conceived and their '*feeling* to the mind' (p. 125). It 'distinguishes the ideas of the judgment from the fictions of the imagination', making them 'the governing principle of our actions' (p. 126). And, if the 'sentiment of belief' is just a 'conception more intense and steady' than that accompanying 'the mere fictions' of the imagination, and which arises from 'customary conjunction' of the object with something 'present to the memory or senses', it should not be hard to find other 'analogous' mental 'operations' (p. 126).

We have reduced the 'principles of connexion', which

'unite our thoughts', to three: '*Resemblance, Contiguity*, and *Causation*' (p. 126). Now, when an object is presented to 'the senses or memory', is the mind not only drawn 'to the conception of the **correlative**', but does it also achieve a 'steadier and stronger conception of it' than it would otherwise (p. 126)? It seems to with the 'belief' that arises from 'cause and effect'; and, if it does with the 'other relations', we may have found a 'general law' of mental operations (p. 126). Let us take the example of '**ROMAN CATHOLIC**' ceremonies (p. 127). Its adherents claim that their 'external motions' enliven 'their devotion', which would slacken if wholly 'directed' to 'distant and immaterial objects': they hold that the '**images**' in their churches make the 'objects' of their faith 'more present' to them (p. 127). This suggests that 'the effect of resemblance in enlivening the ideas is very common' (p. 127).

With '*contiguity*', 'distance diminishes the force of every idea' (p. 127). The 'actual presence of an object' carries the mind to it with 'superior vivacity': when I am close to home, everything about it 'touches me more nearly' than when I am far from it (p. 127). It is the same with 'causation' (p. 128). 'Superstitious people are fond of the **relics** of saints': the best any 'devotee' could obtain would be 'the handywork of a saint' (p. 128). Of course, in all these cases, belief in 'the correlative object is always presupposed': 'contiguity to home' cannot 'excite our ideas' of it, unless 'we *believe*' that 'it really exists' (p. 128). Belief, when it goes 'beyond the memory or senses', arises from 'similar causes' (pp. 128–9). If I throw 'dry wood' on the fire, straight away my mind is drawn to think that it 'augments, not extinguishes the flame' (p. 129). This 'transition of thought' from 'cause to effect' does not come from the reason, but from 'custom and experience'; and, as it starts with an object 'present to the senses', it makes the idea 'of flame' livelier than it could be in the imagination (p. 129). And what is there to cause 'such a strong conception', apart from 'a present object and a customary transition to the idea of another' (p. 129)? This is the whole 'operation of the mind', as it relates to our conclusions about 'matter of fact and existence' (p. 129).

There is a 'kind of pre-established harmony' between 'the course of nature' and the 'succession of our ideas': custom is the 'principle', by which 'this correspondence', so essential to the survival of 'our species', has been 'effected' (p. 129). Without it, our knowledge would be limited to the 'narrow sphere' of 'memory and senses', and we would be unable to use our 'natural powers' to accomplish 'good', or avoid 'evil' (p. 129). Furthermore, this mental operation, of inferring 'like effects from like causes', could not have been entrusted to 'our reason', which is error-prone, and only develops after 'infancy' (pp. 129–30). It is better that it is a 'mechanical' operation, which appears at the start of our lives (p. 130). Nature has 'implanted in us' an instinct, which moves our thoughts in a 'correspondent course' to the one she has 'established among external objects', even though she has not shown us the 'powers and forces' which produce this 'succession of objects' (p. 130).

Section 6
Of Probability (pp. 131–3)

Although there may be 'no such thing as *Chance*', our 'ignorance of the real cause' of events leads to a similar 'species of **belief** or **opinion**' (p. 131). '**Probability**' arises from there being a 'superiority of chances' for one outcome, rather than another (p. 131). If a '**dye**' were marked with 'one figure' on four sides, and a different one on the other two, it would be 'more probable' that the first figure would 'turn up'; and the greater the 'probability', the more 'steady and secure' our belief will be (p. 131). When we think about the result of throwing a dice, we think it equally 'probable' that any side will turn up: this is the 'very nature of chance' (p. 131). But when we know that more sides are marked with one figure than another, the 'mind is carried more frequently to that event', attaching to it the 'sentiment of belief', and giving it 'the advantage over its antagonist' (p. 131). This 'imprints the idea more strongly on the imagination'; gives it a greater 'influence on the passions'; and leads to 'that reliance or security, which constitutes the nature of belief and opinion' (p. 132).

The same is true of the 'probability of causes' (p. 132). Some causes, such as the '**universal law**' of 'gravity', are 'uniform and constant', and have never been known to show any 'irregularity' (p. 132). Others, however, are 'uncertain' in their effects (p. 132). But when a cause does not produce its 'usual effect', this is attributed, not to an 'irregularity in nature', but to the presence of an unknown cause, which is preventing 'the operation' (p. 132). In all 'our inferences', we transfer 'past' to 'future', and, where the former has been 'entirely regular', expect the event to occur 'with the greatest assurance' (p. 132). However, where causes, apparently 'exactly similar', have been found to produce 'different effects', we take this into account when determining the 'probability of the event', giving 'preference' to what is 'most usual' (p. 132). Thus, in European countries, it is more probable that there will be frost 'in JANUARY' than not, but the 'probability varies', according to the countries' 'different climates' (p. 132). In transferring the 'past to the future', we calculate the frequency with which 'different events' have resulted from 'any cause', and expect the event that has occurred most often (p. 132). This produces *'belief'*, giving its 'object the preference above the contrary event' (p. 133).

Section 7
Of the Idea of Necessary Connexion (pp. 134–47)

Part 1 (pp. 134–43)

The 'advantage' of the 'mathematical sciences' over the 'moral' ones is that their 'ideas' are 'clear and determinate' (p. 134). On the other hand, the mathematical sciences involve 'longer and more intricate' chains of reasoning, while, in the **moral sciences**, though their ideas can become obscure and confused, the 'inferences' and 'intermediate steps' are 'shorter' (p. 134). However, lack of progress in them suggests they require 'superior care' (p. 135). In metaphysics, no ideas are more 'obscure and uncertain' than *'power, force, energy,* or **necessary connexion**': here, we shall try to establish the 'precise meaning of these terms' (p. 135).

A non-controversial proposition, which I have tried to explain above, is that 'our ideas' are 'copies of our impressions': we cannot *'think'* of anything that our 'external or internal senses' have not previously *'felt'* (p. 135). **'Complex ideas'** may be known 'by definition', but this just enumerates the 'simple ideas' of which they consist (p. 135). But what if there is 'ambiguity' in the 'most simple ideas' (p. 135)? We must produce 'the impressions', from which 'the ideas are copied', which may 'throw light' on them (p. 136). To become 'fully acquainted' with 'necessary connexion', we must 'examine its impression' in the 'sources' from which it derives (p. 136).

With 'external objects', if our minds could discover the 'power' of any cause, we would be able to 'foresee' its 'effect'

(p. 136). However, we have no '*inward* impression' of a 'necessary connexion', binding cause and effect, such that the second is the 'infallible consequence' of the first; it is just apparent, to our '*outward* senses', that one follows the other: heat always accompanies flame, but we do not know what connects them (pp. 136–7). But we are aware of the 'internal power', by which 'command' is exercised by will, both over 'the organs of the body' and the 'faculties of the soul' (p. 137). Perhaps, we can derive the idea of necessary connexion from reflection on 'the operations of our own mind' (p. 137)? But, although we are always 'conscious' that bodily motion follows 'volition', we cannot find out how our will carries out this 'operation' (p. 137). For, '*first*', nothing 'in all nature' is 'more mysterious' than the 'union of soul with body', which gives 'supposed spiritual substance' such 'influence' over 'a material one' (p. 137). '*Secondly*', we do not know why we are able to 'move' some bodily organs, such as the 'tongue and fingers', but not others, such as 'the heart or liver' (p. 138). We 'learn the influence of our will from experience alone', which shows us that one 'event constantly follows another', but not the 'secret connexion' that 'binds them together' (p. 138). '*Thirdly*', anatomy tells us that the 'immediate object of power in voluntary motion' is not the 'member itself', but 'muscles, and nerves' (p. 138). Thus, the 'desired event' is produced as a result of 'a long succession' of others, showing how 'mysterious' the process is: the power by which we move our limbs is 'wholly beyond our comprehension' (pp. 138–9).

Can we claim to be 'conscious of a power' in 'our own minds', when, by an 'act' of will, we bring to our minds, and contemplate, 'a new idea' (p. 139)? It seems not. '*First*', to 'know a power', we must know how a particular cause produces its effect, but we cannot 'pretend to be acquainted' with

43

the 'nature of the **human soul**', that of an idea, or how one produces the other (p. 139). We just experience 'the event', the existence of the idea, but do not understand how 'it is produced' (p. 140). '*Secondly*', mind's command 'over itself is limited' (for example, we have more 'authority' over 'our ideas' than our 'passions'): but we know these limits through 'experience and observation', not 'reason' (p. 140). '*Thirdly*', our 'self-command' is greater at some times than others: we are more 'master of our thoughts' in the morning than the evening (p. 140). However, we can give no 'reason for these variations', apart from experience (p. 140). Thus, so far from understanding the 'energy of the will', we need experience to convince us that such effects can be produced by 'a simple act of volition' (p. 140).

The 'generality of mankind' has no 'difficulty' explaining the 'familiar operations of nature', such as plant growth or the 'generation of animals': by 'long habit', on 'appearance of the cause', they expect its 'usual' effect (p. 140). But when extra-ordinary events, like 'earthquakes', occur, they are unable to find a cause for it in the 'common powers of nature', and fall back on 'some **invisible intelligent principle**' as its cause (p. 141). Philosophers, who enquire into matters rather further, recognize that the cause of even 'familiar events' is 'unintelligible' (p. 141). Some of them then argue (as the 'vulgar' do only with extraordinary events) that the 'true and direct' cause of 'every effect' does not lie in nature, but in 'a volition of the Supreme Being', who, according to the '**general laws**' of 'the universe' he has laid down, wills that certain objects should always 'be conjoined' (p. 141). And, seeing that we do not understand how mind affects body, they also assert that God causes 'the union between soul and body', and that it is a divine 'volition', not our senses, which produces 'sensations'

44

of external objects 'in the mind' and 'motion in our members' (pp. 141–2). Some even say that our 'conception of ideas' is 'a revelation', made to us by God (p. 142). They think that, by doing so, they are 'magnifying' the 'grandeur' of God's '**attributes**' (p. 142). However, it argues 'more power' in God that he should be able to make a world, which, by its 'proper operation', fulfils all his 'purposes', than that he should need to be 'obliged every moment' to intervene, and '**adjust its parts**' (p. 142). Further, *'first'*, such a 'theory' carries us 'beyond the reach of our faculties': it is outside the 'sphere of experience', and we are in 'fairy land' long before we get to its 'last steps' (pp. 142–3). '*Secondly*', we are 'ignorant' of how 'a mind, even the supreme mind', operates, and have 'no idea of the Supreme Being', apart from 'reflection on our own faculties' (p. 143).

Part 2 (pp. 143–7)

To bring this 'argument' to a conclusion: we have searched 'in vain' for an idea of 'necessary connexion', but can only find 'one event following another', without any connection of 'cause' and 'effect' (pp. 143–4). All events seem 'loose and separate'; they are *'conjoined, but never connected'* (p. 144). However, although observing 'a particular event' following another does not entitle us to 'form a general rule', or foretell what will happen 'in like cases', when a whole 'species of event' has always been 'conjoined with another', we do not hesitate to call one *'Cause'* and the other, *'Effect'* (p. 144). We take it that one 'infallibly produces the other' (p. 144). Thus, it is from 'habit', the connection 'we *feel* in the mind', that we 'form the idea' of 'necessary connexion' (p. 145). When the 'communication of motion by impulse', as in 'two billiard-balls' colliding, has been observed many times, we declare them to be *'connected'*

(p. 145). Saying two objects are thus 'connected' means they have 'acquired a connexion in our thought' (p. 145).

This shows the 'weakness of the understanding' (p. 145). We need to know about 'cause and effect', as all 'our reasonings' about 'fact or existence' are based on it: the only 'immediate utility' of the sciences is to teach us how to 'controul and regulate future events by their causes' (p. 145). But we cannot give a satisfactory 'definition of *cause*': from experience, we can only say that a cause is '*an object, followed by another, and where all the objects, similar to the first, are followed by objects similar to the second*'; and '*an object followed by another, and whose appearance always conveys the thought to that other*' (p. 146). We have no 'more perfect definition' (p. 146). So, nothing 'produces any impression', or suggests 'any idea', of 'necessary connexion'; but, when there are 'many uniform instances' of the 'same event' following 'the same object', we 'begin to entertain the notion of cause and connexion' (p. 147). We '*feel* a new sentiment or impression': a 'customary connexion in the thought or imagination between one object and its usual attendant' (p. 147).

Section 8
Of Liberty and Necessity (pp. 148–64)

Part 1 (pp. 148–59)

It would be thought that, with 'questions' that have been eagerly discussed for 'two thousand years', there would be agreement about the 'exact definitions of the terms' (p. 148). But the 'opposite' may be the case: 'ambiguity' in the terms, and 'disputants' attaching 'different ideas' to them, may be the reason why a 'controversy' persists for so long (p. 148).

This is the case with the issue of '**liberty** and **necessity**', where we shall probably find that both the 'learned and ignorant' are actually of 'the same opinion', and that 'a few intelligible definitions' would 'put an end to the whole controversy' (pp. 148–9). Indeed, I hope to show that 'all men' have always had the same view 'of necessity and of liberty', and that the whole issue has 'turned merely upon words' (p. 149).

We shall start with 'the **doctrine of necessity**' (p. 149). It is 'universally allowed' that the 'laws of nature' exactly prescribe the 'degree and direction of every motion' (p. 149). If everything in nature were always changing, so that 'no two events' resembled each other, and 'every object was entirely new', we would have no idea 'of necessity and causation', which arise from 'uniformity' in the 'operations of nature': it is the 'constant *conjunction* of similar objects', and the 'consequent *inference* from one to the other', which gives us the 'notion' of 'necessity' and 'connexion' (pp. 149–50). If it appears we have always accepted that these apply to the 'voluntary actions of men', it follows that they 'have ever agreed in the doctrine of necessity', and any dispute about it results from their not 'understanding each other' (p. 150).

It is generally agreed that 'human nature' remains the same across the ages: the 'same motives', such as 'ambition, **avarice**, self-love', always produce the same actions (p. 150). If we want to know what the 'GREEKS and ROMANS' were like, we should study 'the temper and actions of the FRENCH and ENGLISH' (p. 150). We can regard all the 'wars, intrigues' and 'revolutions' that have taken place as 'so many collections of experiments', which enable us to 'discover the constant and universal principles of human nature' (p. 150). If a 'traveller' returned from a distant country with stories of people, who were motivated entirely by 'friendship, generosity, and public spirit', we would know he was lying, just as certainly as if he had told us stories of '**centaurs** and dragons' (p. 151). The experience we acquire, during life and through mixing with different people, instructs us in 'the principles of human nature' (p. 151). While we still expect to encounter 'virtue and honour', we do not expect to find 'perfect disinterestedness', either 'in multitudes' or 'in individuals of any rank' (p. 151). If there were 'no uniformity in human actions', no experience could 'ever serve to any purpose' (p. 151).

This is not to say that human beings 'always act precisely in the same manner' (p. 152). We must allow for 'diversity' of character and opinion: absolute 'uniformity' is not found in any 'part of nature' (p. 152). There are also differences be-tween 'ages and countries', 'the sexes', and people at 'different periods' of life (p. 152). We must also be aware that not all causes are 'conjoined to their usual effects, with like uniform-ity' (p 152). Ordinary people always 'attribute the uncertainty of events' to 'uncertainty in the causes', but philosophers realize that 'the connexion between all causes and effects is equally necessary', and that 'seeming uncertainty' is the result of 'the secret opposition of contrary causes' (pp. 152–3). A 'peasant' thinks a clock keeps stopping, because it does not 'go right', but one who understands clocks sees that, although the mechanism continues to operate in the same way, a 'grain of dust' is stopping 'the whole movement' (p. 153). Similarly, 'the philosopher and physician' recognize that the 'human body is a mighty complicated machine', with 'many secret powers': what seem to be 'irregular events' do not prove that 'the laws of nature are not observed with the greatest regular-ity' (p. 153).

Therefore, those who know every 'circumstance' of 'char-acter and situation' may be able to explain human beings' apparently 'irregular and unexpected resolutions' (p. 153). A usually 'obliging' person is 'peevish': but he has 'toothake' (p. 153). Human 'motives' operate uniformly, 'notwithstanding these seeming irregularities' (p. 154). This 'regular conjunction' between 'motives and voluntary actions' is 'universally acknowledged', and enables us to 'draw *inferences*' about 'human actions' (p. 154). As society becomes more 'complicated', the 'variety of voluntary actions' may increase, but, on the basis of 'past experience', we expect people, as well as 'external objects', to continue to operate in the same way as previously (p. 154). A 'manufacturer' thinks he can depend on 'the labour of his servants', just as much as 'upon the tools' (p. 154). Thus, everyone, including 'philosophers', accepts the 'doctrine of necessity' (pp. 154–5). There could be no 'science' of '*politics*', if 'laws and forms of government' did not influence society uniformly, or 'foundation of *morals*', if 'particular characters' had no 'certain' power to 'produce particular sentiments', which have a 'constant' effect 'on actions' (p. 155). A prisoner, with 'neither money nor interest', knows that the 'obstinacy of the gaoler' is as much an obstacle to escape as 'walls and bars' (p. 155). I know that it is no more likely that my 'honest and opulent' friend will 'come into my house' to rob me than that the house itself will fall down: unless, of course, he is '*seized with a sudden and unknown frenzy*' (p. 156). On the other hand, one who leaves his 'purse full of gold', on the pavement 'at Charing Cross', is as likely to find it there 'an hour after', as to see it flying away 'like a feather' (p. 156).

We accept 'the doctrine of necessity', so why are we reluctant to 'acknowledge it in words' (p. 156)? I think it is because what we observe is that 'particular objects are *constantly conjoined*', and, on this basis, we conclude that there is 'a necessary connexion between the cause and the effect' (p. 156). But, when we turn to the 'operations' of our 'own minds', we do not '*feel*' the same connection between 'the motive and the action', and think that effects, brought about by 'thought and intelligence', are different from those resulting from 'material force' (pp. 156–7). But, once we see that 'the *constant conjunction* of objects' also applies to 'voluntary actions', we shall be able to accept that they have 'the same necessity common to all causes' (p. 157). Ascribing 'necessity to the determinations of the will' may 'contradict' certain philosophical systems, but any 'dissent' is merely a matter of words (p. 157). When we start by examining 'the faculties of the soul', we begin 'at the wrong end of this question' (p. 157). We tend to think that, with 'external objects', there is 'some farther idea of necessity and causation', which is not present in 'the voluntary actions of the mind'; and this stops us 'bringing the question to any determinate issue' (p. 157). The fact is that all we know of 'material causes' is 'constant conjunction and inference' (p. 157). It may seem unappealing to 'fix such narrow limits to human understanding', but we can and do apply it to human beings, for we always 'draw inferences' between human actions and motives (p. 158).

How do we reconcile 'liberty and necessity' (p. 158)? The whole question is 'merely verbal' (p. 158). We cannot deny that actions are connected with motives, or that one follows 'with a certain degree of uniformity from the other' (pp. 158–9). By '*liberty*', we mean '*a **power of acting or not acting, according to the determinations of the will**' (p. 159). Apart from one who is 'a prisoner and in chains', everyone is acknowledged to possess such liberty (p. 159). Our definition of '*liberty*' must be consistent both 'with plain matter of fact' and 'with itself' (p. 159). Nothing 'exists without a cause of its existence' (p. 159). Now, if anyone can define cause, without including '*necessary con-*

nexion with its effect', I shall give up this 'controversy', for, unless objects had 'a regular conjunction with each other', we would have no 'notion of cause and effect' (p. 159). If my definition 'be admitted', liberty, 'when opposed to necessity, not to **constraint**', must be 'universally allowed to have no existence' (p. 159).

Part 2 (pp. 160–4)

In philosophy, no 'method of reasoning' is more 'blameable' than trying to refute a 'hypothesis', by claiming that it will have 'dangerous consequences to religion and morality' (p. 160). Further, as 'above explained', the doctrines of 'necessity and of liberty', as well as being 'consistent with morality', are 'essential to its support' (p. 160). There are two ways of defining *'cause'*: the 'constant conjunction of like objects' or 'the inference of the understanding from one object to another' (p. 160). 'Necessity', in both 'senses', has been 'universally' regarded as belonging to 'the will of man', and no one has tried to deny (although some may refuse to describe it as *'necessity'*) our ability to 'draw inferences concerning human actions', or that these are based on the 'experienced union of like actions, with like motives' (p. 160). Nothing is more 'innocent' than this doctrine, which, whatever its implications for 'natural philosophy or metaphysics', has none for 'morality or religion' (p. 160). All laws are 'founded on rewards and punishments', which 'influence' the mind, producing 'good' and preventing 'evil actions'; and this is considered 'an instance of that necessity' we are trying to establish (pp. 160–1).

Only one who possesses 'thought and consciousness' can be a 'proper object of hatred or vengeance' (p. 161). Unless actions 'proceed' from 'some *cause*' in the 'character and disposition' of the person who 'performed them', he cannot be praised or blamed for them, even if they break 'all the rules of morality and religion' (p. 161). Without 'necessity, and consequently causes', a person could commit the 'most horrid crime', and still be blameless (p. 161). We do not blame people for actions they 'perform ignorantly', but condemn them for bad actions that 'proceed from deliberation', because these prove 'criminal principles in the mind' (p. 161). The 'same arguments' prove that *'liberty'* is also 'essential to morality': we cannot hold people accountable for things they do as a result of 'external violence' (pp. 161–2).

Now, 'I can foresee other objections' (p. 162). It may be argued that, if the 'laws of necessity' apply to 'voluntary actions', there must be a 'chain of necessary causes', so every human '**volition**' has been '**pre-ordained and pre-determined**' by the 'original cause of all'; and, therefore, either human beings are not responsible for their actions, or 'the same guilt' attaches to 'our **Creator**' (p. 162). An 'infinitely wise and powerful' being, he must have foreseen and 'intended all those actions of men', which we 'pronounce criminal' (p. 162). So, either they are not criminal, in view of the 'infinite perfection' of the being from whom they derive, or, if they are criminal, as God, 'not man', is responsible for them, we must not ascribe 'the attribute of perfection' to him (pp. 162–3). However, both these 'positions' are 'absurd and impious', and so 'cannot possibly be true' (p. 162).

With the first, although some philosophers have contended that the world, 'considered as one system', is 'ordered with perfect **benevolence**', and that every apparent '**physical ill**' is, 'in reality', good, the argument is not convincing (p. 163). It may satisfy someone living in 'ease and security', but will be dismissed by someone suffering the 'pains of the gout' (p. 163).

As for *'moral'* **ills**, human beings are so 'formed by nature' that they 'immediately' feel 'approbation or blame' for certain kinds of character or action, commending those that contribute to society's 'peace and security' and condemning those that 'tend to public detriment' (pp. 163–4). No amount of 'philosophical theory or speculation' is going to persuade people to change their view of 'vice and virtue': they will not persuade a person, who has been 'robbed of a considerable sum', that he should stop being angry about it (p. 164). With the second, it is more difficult to see how God can be the **'mediate cause'** of all human actions, without being the 'author of **sin**': reconciling the **'indifference and contingency of human actions** with **prescience'** is beyond 'the power of philosophy' (p. 164). It is better to confine our enquiries to 'examination of common life' than to launch into 'so boundless an ocean of doubt, uncertainty and contradiction' (p. 164).

Section 9
Of the Reason of Animals (pp. 165–8)

Our 'reasonings' about matters of fact are based on a type of **'ANALOGY'**: we expect a cause to produce the same effects as 'similar' ones we have seen (p. 165). Where the causes are 'entirely similar', the analogy is 'perfect', and the **'inference'** drawn is 'conclusive', but where the objects resemble each other less closely, the analogy is 'less perfect', so the inference has less 'force': how much it has depends on the 'degree of similarity and resemblance' (p. 165). We extend the 'anatomical observations' we make, in relation to one type of animal, to others: when we find 'circulation of the blood' in one, we expect to find it in the rest (p. 165). We can take our 'analogical observations' further (p. 165). It will add weight to our theory about how the human understanding and 'passions' operate, if it is found to explain 'the same phaenomena' in animals (p. 165). They also learn 'from experience', and conclude that the 'same causes' will produce the same results (p. 165). This is how they become familiar with the 'nature' and 'effects' of 'fire, water, earth' and so on (p. 165). For example, a horse that is used 'to the field' knows which objects 'he can leap' (p. 166). Animals can be taught to do things, including those that are 'contrary to their natural instincts', by use of 'rewards and punishments' (p. 166). It is experience that makes a dog 'answer to his name', when you utter that particular sound in 'a certain tone' (p. 166). The animal's 'inference' is based on 'past experience': it expects the 'same consequences' to flow from 'similar objects' (p. 166).

The animal's inference cannot be based on 'reasoning', as it lacks this ability (p. 166). And, indeed, even philosophers do not employ reason 'in all the active parts of life' (p. 166). Nature must have 'provided' some other means to make it possible to infer effects from causes (p. 166). It is 'custom alone', which enables animals to infer one thing from another, and which leads their 'imagination' from the 'appearance of the one, to conceive the other' in that 'particular manner' we call *'belief'* (p. 167). However, although animals acquire knowledge from 'observation', they also 'derive' it from the 'original hand of nature' (p. 167). We call these *'instincts'* (p. 167). And, indeed, the 'experimental reasoning', which we share with animals, is a type of 'instinct', the 'operations' of which, in us, are not governed by our 'intellectual faculties' (p. 168). Instinct teaches human beings to 'avoid the fire', as it does birds the 'art of incubation' (p. 168).

Section 10
Of Miracles (pp. 169–86)

Part 1 (pp. 169–73)

Tillotson has a powerful argument against 'the *real presence*' (p. 169). The 'authority' of 'scripture' and the Christian 'tradition' is based on the 'testimony of the **apostles**', who were 'eyewitnesses' to Jesus' miracles (p. 169). Thus, the 'evidence' for Christianity's 'truth' is less than that for 'the truth of our senses', as it was 'no greater', even for those who started the 'religion', and no one should place as much 'confidence' in others' 'testimony' as in things he sees himself (p. 169). So, however 'clearly' the 'real presence' was '**revealed** in scripture', it would break the 'rules of just reasoning' to believe in it, as it 'contradicts' sense experience; and the evidence of scriptural revelation is not as powerful as that of 'sense', except when reinforced by 'the **Holy Spirit**' (p. 169). I believe I have found an equally 'decisive argument' against 'all kinds of **superstitious delusion**', such as '**miracles**' (p. 169).

Although 'experience' is our 'only guide' concerning 'matters of fact', because not all effects follow 'with like certainty from their supposed causes', it is prone to error (pp. 169–70). Some events are 'constantly conjoined together', but the conjunction of others is 'more variable', and may 'disappoint our expectations' (p. 170). The 'wise man', therefore, 'proportions his belief to the evidence' (p. 170). In some cases, on the basis of 'past experience', he expects the event with the 'last degree of assurance'; in others, he has to weigh conflicting evidence, and then, with 'doubt and hesitation', make a 'judgment' on the basis of '*probability*' (p. 170). A 'hundred instances', on 'one side', against 'fifty on another', give a 'doubtful expectation of any event', but a 'hundred uniform experiments', against a single 'contradictory' one, produce a 'strong degree of assurance' (p. 170).

Let us 'apply these principles' to a 'particular' case (p. 170). No type of 'reasoning' is 'more useful' than that based on eye-witness 'reports' (p. 170). This is because we have found people to be generally truthful: usually, there is 'conformity of facts to the reports of witnesses' (p. 170). However, as it is a 'general maxim' that no two objects have a 'discoverable connexion' with one another, and that all our 'inferences' from one to the other are based on experience, we must not make 'an exception' of 'human testimony' (pp. 170–1). After all, had we not discovered, 'by *experience*', an 'inclination to truth' in 'human nature', we would not have 'confidence in human testimony'. Now, whether the 'evidence' from 'human testimony' is regarded as 'a *proof* or a *probability*' depends on the degree to which experience shows the 'conjunction' between 'any particular kind of report and any kind of object' to be 'constant or variable' (p. 171). 'Experience and observation' are always the 'ultimate standard', against which we measure human testimony; and we may have reasons to doubt particular testimony, as when witnesses 'contradict each other', they are of 'doubtful character', or have 'an interest in what they affirm' (p. 171).

If the testimony is trying to establish the 'extraordinary and the marvellous', its force is diminished, 'in proportion', as it is 'more or less unusual' (pp. 171–2). We believe 'witnesses and historians', not because we see an '*a priori*' connection between 'testimony and reality', but because we are 'accustomed to find a conformity between them' (p. 172). However, when the 'fact attested' is one that is 'seldom' observed, our 'experiences' conflict, so that very 'principle of experience', which generally inclines us to trust the 'testimony of witnesses', leads us to doubt it (p. 172). The 'INDIAN prince', who doubted reports about 'the effects of frost, reasoned justly': the reports were at odds with 'events, of which he had had constant and uniform experience' (p. 172).

To increase the 'probability' against the testimony of witnesses, let us suppose they are affirming something, not 'only marvellous', but 'miraculous' (pp. 172–3). A miracle is a '**violation of the laws of nature**': as these have been established by 'unalterable experience', they are as powerful a 'proof against a miracle' as can 'be imagined' (p. 173). After all, why is it 'more than probable' that human beings 'must die', or that 'fire consumes wood' (p. 173)? It is because these events conform to 'the laws of nature', and it would require a 'violation' of the latter, or a miracle, to 'prevent them' (p. 173). Nothing is called 'a miracle', if it happens in the 'common course of nature', which means that 'uniform experience' is against miraculous events (p. 173). And, as 'uniform experience' is 'a proof', there is thus 'direct and full *proof*' against 'any miracle' (p. 173). What all this means is that no testimony is 'sufficient to establish a miracle', unless its not being true would be 'more miraculous' than the miracle it seeks to establish (pp. 173–4). If someone tells me he saw a 'dead man restored to life', I ask which is 'more probable': that the event should actually 'have happened', or that the witness should 'deceive or be deceived'; and I 'always reject the greater miracle' (p. 174). He would only convince me if the 'falsehood of his testimony' were 'more miraculous' than the event he described (p. 174).

Part 2 (pp. 174–86)

Furthermore, *'first'*, there is not 'in all history' any miracle, 'attested' by a 'sufficient number' of people of 'undoubted integrity', to assure us that they were not under a 'delusion', or intending 'to deceive others' (p. 174). '*Secondly*', there is an element in 'human nature', which reduces any credit we should give to 'testimony' about miracles (p. 174). Generally, we proceed on the basis that what has been 'found to be most usual is always most probable' and, where accounts of an event differ, refer to 'past observations' to decide what happened (pp. 174–5). But when something is 'utterly absurd and miraculous', there is a tendency to believe it, due to the 'agreeable' nature of the '*surprize* and *wonder*' associated with 'miraculous events' (p. 175). Look at the eagerness with which people listen to travellers' tales of 'sea and land monsters' (p. 175). If 'the spirit of religion' joins with 'love of wonder', that is the 'end of common sense' (p. 175). A **'religionist'** may be 'an enthusiast', who imagines 'he sees what has no reality'; but his **'auditors'** often lack 'sufficient judgment' to challenge his 'evidence', and, if he tells his story eloquently, he will give them little room for 'reason or reflection' (p. 175). All the **'forged miracles'** that have been 'detected' by 'contrary evidence', or shown for what they are by 'their absurdity', prove human beings' 'propensity' for 'the extraordinary and the marvellous' (pp. 175–6). We delight in relating an interesting 'piece of news': the 'same passions' incline us to 'believe and report', with complete conviction, 'all religious miracles' (p. 176).

'*Thirdly*', it is a 'strong presumption' against accounts of miracles that they occur 'among ignorant and barbarous nations', or, if the nation is 'civilized', have been 'transmitted' by 'ignorant and barbarous ancestors' (p. 176). The 'first histories of all nations' show a very different attitude towards 'nature' from the one we have today (p. 176). 'Battles' and 'famine' never result from 'natural causes', but are associated with '**omens**' and '**oracles**'; but these stories diminish as 'we advance nearer the enlightened ages' (p. 176). As '**LUCIAN**' recounts, the 'false prophet, **ALEXANDER**', was wise to begin 'his impostures' among the 'ignorant **PAPHLAGONIANS**' (p. 177). 'Fools are industrious' in spreading such stories, while the 'wise and learned' dismiss them, without finding out all the 'particular facts', so as to be able to refute them in detail (p. 177). As a result, Alexander was able to gain a following even among '**GRECIAN** philosophers', and to attract 'the attention' of the 'emperor **MARCUS AURELIUS**' (p. 177). Such 'an imposture' has a far greater chance of succeeding in 'remote countries', among 'ignorant people', than in a 'city renowned for arts and knowledge' (p. 177). If Alexander had been based in '**ATHENS**', its 'philosophers' would soon have used their 'reason and eloquence' to open 'the eyes of mankind' (p. 177). Lucian was able to do so, but unfortunately, not 'every ALEXANDER meets with a LUCIAN' (pp. 177–8).

A '*fourth* reason' against such '**prodigies**' is that even those, which have not been clearly proved false, are 'opposed by an infinite number of witnesses' (p. 178). In 'matters of religion', that which is 'different is contrary', so the different religions of 'ancient ROME', 'TURKEY' and '**SIAM**' cannot all have a 'solid foundation' (p. 178). Any miracle, claimed by one of them, has the indirect effect of overthrowing the others: the miracles of 'different religions' should be seen as 'contrary facts' and 'opposite to each other' (p. 178). When 'authors and witnesses' recount a 'miracle in their particular religion', we should treat their account as if it referred to one in another religion, and 'in express terms contradicted it' (p. 178). A story '**CARDINAL DE RETZ**' tells, about an experience he had in '**SARAGOSSA**', merits our attention (p. 179). In the cathedral, he met 'a door-keeper' who had lost a leg, but who, it was claimed, had 'recovered' it by 'rubbing of holy oil upon the stump' (p. 179). This miracle was generally accepted in the town, and 'vouched by all the **canons** of the church' (p. 179). But the cardinal did not 'give any credit to it' (p. 179). He did not think it necessary or possible to 'be able accurately to disprove the testimony' he had heard; rather, 'like a just reasoner', he held that the 'evidence carried falsehood' on its 'very face' (pp. 179–80). Numerous miracles, such as restoring 'hearing to the deaf, and sight to the blind', were said to have been 'wrought' on the 'tomb of **Abbé PARIS, the famous JANSENIST**'; and these were 'attested by witnesses of credit' (p. 180). What do we have to 'oppose to such a cloud of witnesses' (pp. 180–1)? We have the 'absolute impossibility' of these miracles, which 'all reasonable people' will consider 'sufficient refutation' (p. 181).

The fact that human testimony has 'the utmost force and authority in some cases' does not mean that it has 'equal force and authority' in all (p. 182). The 'wise' treat with caution any report that 'favours' the reporter by, for example, promoting 'his family, or himself' (p. 182). It is an even 'greater temptation' to appear as a 'missionary' or 'prophet' from 'heaven', while the 'gazing populace' is ever eager to receive uncritically 'whatever sooths superstition, and promotes wonder' (pp. 182–3). When reports of miracles 'fly about', we must treat them as instances of 'credulity and delusion', not believe there has been a 'miraculous violation' of 'established laws of nature' (p. 183). By doing so, we judge them on the basis of our 'regular experience and observation' (p. 183). Even in a '**court of judicature**', it is often hard to 'distinguish between truth and falsehood' (p. 183). The 'learned' tend to ignore the claims of 'new religions', until it is too late to 'un-deceive the deluded multitude', who are incapable of seeing the reporters' 'testimony' for what it is (p. 183).

But 'no testimony' for any miracle has ever 'amounted to a probability', much less 'a proof' (p. 183). Only experience can give 'authority' to 'human testimony', but experience 'assures us of the laws of nature' (p. 184). When 'these two kinds of experience are contrary', it means 'entire annihilation' of the claims of 'popular religions' (p. 184).

Thus, we can take it as 'a maxim' that no testimony can 'prove a miracle', or establish it as the basis for any 'system of religion' (p. 184). But it is important to understand what is meant by 'a miracle' (p. 184). If 'all authors, in all languages' agreed, without 'variation or contradiction', that, on 'the first of JANUARY 1600', the earth was in 'total darkness' for eight days, then 'present philosophers' should not doubt it, but start to 'search for the causes' (p. 184). There is, after all, plenty of evidence of nature's 'corruption, and dissolution' (p. 184). But, if 'all the historians' of **Queen Elizabeth's** reign stated that she died on 1 January 1600, but, after 'being interred a month', returned to life, and 'governed ENGLAND for three years', I would not 'believe so miraculous an event' (p. 184). However powerful the evidence, I would not accept 'so signal a violation of the laws of nature' (p. 185).

Through the ages, people have been 'imposed on by ridiculous stories of that kind' (p. 185). Even if a miracle is 'ascribed' to the '**Almighty**', this does not make it any more 'probable', as we cannot know 'the attributes or actions of such a Being', apart from our **experience of 'his productions, in the usual course of nature'** (p. 185). This just brings us back to 'past observation': we must compare examples of people's 'violations of truth' in what they say with violations of natural laws by alleged miracles, and 'judge' which is most 'probable' (p. 185). '**BACON**' used the 'same principles of reasoning', when he urged us to scrutinize every claim about something 'new, rare, and extraordinary in nature', particularly if it depends on 'religion', as those who write about such things have an 'unconquerable appetite for falsehood and fable' (p. 185). This 'method of reasoning' seems a more effective way of defending 'the CHRISTIAN religion', which is based 'on *Faith*', than 'human reason' (pp. 185–6). Let us examine the miracles we find in scripture, not as the 'testimony of God', but as 'the production of a mere human writer' (p. 186). They appear in a book, full of 'prodigies and miracles', produced by a 'barbarous and ignorant people', whose view of 'the world and of human nature' differs markedly from ours (p. 186). Can anyone honestly 'declare' the 'falsehood' of such a book to be more 'miraculous' than 'the miracles it relates' (p. 186)? Yet, it must be to meet the 'measures of probability' we established previously (p. 186). And what we have said of miracles applies without 'variation to prophecies' (p. 186). Our conclusion must be that Christianity was not only 'at first attended with miracles', but cannot be believed by a 'reasonable person' today without one: reason is 'insufficient' to convince us of its truth (p. 186). Whoever is 'moved by *Faith*' to accept it is aware of a 'continued miracle in his own person', which overcomes 'all the principles of his understanding', and enables him to believe what is 'most contrary to custom and experience' (p. 186).

Section 11
Of a Particular Providence and of a Future State
(pp. 187–98)

I was talking to a friend recently, and pointed out philosophy's 'singular good fortune' to have begun in an '**age and country**', where it was given the 'freedom' it needs to flourish (p. 187). Apart from the 'banishment of **PROTAGORAS**' and the 'death of **SOCRATES**', the 'bigotted jealousy' of the 'present age' was absent (p. 187). Even '**EPICURUS**' was able to live 'in peace' in Athens, while the 'ROMAN emperors' encouraged 'professors' of all types of philosophy, by giving them 'pensions and salaries' (p. 187). But my friend argued that the 'bigotry' I thought 'fatal to philosophy' was actually 'her offspring', which had then joined with 'superstition', and become philosophy's 'persecutor' (p. 188). 'Speculative' religious '**dogmas**' could not be 'conceived' in an 'illiterate' society, where religion matched the 'weak apprehension' of its members (p. 188). What had happened in 'the ages of antiquity' was that, after initial clashes, harmonious relations had developed between philosophy and the '**established super-stition**', with the former attracting the 'learned and wise' and the latter the '**vulgar** and illiterate' (p. 188).

I contended that this argument left out 'politics' (p. 188). Those in charge of society might seek to suppress the views of a philosopher like Epicurus, because his denial of 'divine existence' and a future life could undermine 'morality' (p. 188). My friend replied that 'persecutions' were always caused by 'passion and prejudice', not experience of the ill effects of particular philosophical doctrines (p. 188). He also thought Epicurus could have defended himself successfully, and proved that his philosophical principles were just 'as salutary' as those of 'his adversaries' (p. 188). I urged him to 'make a speech for EPICURUS', in which he addressed, not Athens' 'mob', but its 'philosophical' citizens, and he agreed (p. 188).

Athenians (he declared), I am being censured by 'furious antagonists'; as a result, you have to turn aside from 'questions of public good' to consider issues of 'speculative philosophy' (p. 189). Today, I do not wish to 'dispute' the 'origin and government of worlds', but to establish whether discussing 'such questions' harms 'the public interest' (p. 189). If I can convince you it does not, I hope you will send us back to 'our schools', to pursue our philosophical enquiries (p. 189). Present-day 'religious philosophers', not content with the **religious 'tradition of your forefathers'** (which I accept), want to base 'religion upon the principles of reason' (p. 189). They point to the 'order, beauty, and wise arrangement of the universe', and ask if mere 'chance' could have produced it (p. 189). I am not going to challenge the 'justness of this argument', but, on the basis of 'this very reasoning', show that the issue is a 'speculative' one, and that when 'I deny a **providence** and a future state', I am not undermining society, but putting forward 'principles', which, if my opponents argued 'consistently', they would have to accept as 'solid' (p. 189).

My 'accusers' accept that the main 'argument for a divine existence' comes from the 'order of nature': its 'marks' of '**design**' make it difficult to ascribe its cause to 'chance' (p. 189). This is an argument from 'effects to causes': from the 'order of the work', they infer 'forethought in the workman' (pp. 189–90). But when we infer a 'cause from an effect', we can only ascribe to the former the 'qualities' that are 'sufficient to produce the effect' (p. 190). If a ten-ounce body is raised in a scale, this proves the 'counter-balancing weight' is more than 'ten ounces', but not more than 'a hundred' (p. 190). Ascribing additional qualities to the inferred cause, or saying it is 'capable of producing other effects', is 'conjecture' (p. 190). If a cause is known only by its effect, we can only ascribe to it the qualities needed 'to produce the effect'; we cannot take the cause, and infer 'other effects from it, beyond those by which alone it is known to us' (p. 190). If the gods are the 'authors' of the universe's 'existence or order', it follows that they have the 'precise degree of power, intelligence, and benevolence, which appears in their workmanship' (p. 190). No further attributes 'can ever be proved' (p. 190). We cannot go from 'the universe, the effect, to **JUPITER**, the cause', and then 'descend downwards', and infer 'new' effects from that cause (p. 191). You observe certain phenomena 'in nature', and seek 'a cause' (p. 191). Having found one, you then forget that this 'superlative' being is the 'offspring' of your own minds, and argue that he must be able to produce something 'more perfect' than the present universe, which is 'full of ill and disorder' (p. 191). Philosophers, 'your gods' must be 'suited to the present appearances of nature' (p. 191).

Athenians, when 'priests and poets' complain of the 'vice and misery' of the present age, I hear them with respect, but when philosophers who 'cultivate reason' do so, I do not (p. 191). I ask, 'who admitted them into the councils of the gods', and on what authority do they claim that 'their deities' can or will carry out 'any purpose beyond what has actually appeared' (p. 191)? If they claim they are drawing 'inferences from effects to causes', I point out that they have changed 'their manner of inference', and are actually arguing from 'causes to effects' (p. 191). They are 'presuming' that a 'more perfect' world than the present one is 'more suitable' to their 'perfect' gods, forgetting they have no reason to ascribe to the gods 'any perfection' not 'found' in this one (p. 191). Philosophers argue that the 'qualities of matter', or the 'general laws' of nature, constrained the 'power and benevolence of JUPITER', causing him to create a world containing '**evil and disorder**' and thus 'imperfect' and 'unhappy' human beings (p. 192). But why should it be taken 'for granted' that Jupiter is powerful and benevolent (p. 192)? The 'religious **hypothesis**' is just one way of accounting for what we see in 'the universe' (p. 192). If you think the 'appearances of things' proves a divine cause, you are entitled to infer its existence (p. 192). But, if you argue from 'your inferred causes' that something else has existed, or will exist, in nature, which will provide a 'fuller display' of this divine cause's 'attributes', you depart from your 'method of reasoning' (p. 192). You cannot 'add any thing to the effect', to make it 'more worthy of the cause' (p. 192).

So, how does what I teach imperil 'the security of good morals' (p. 192)? You accuse me of denying that there is a 'supreme governor of the world', who 'punishes the vicious' and 'rewards the virtuous', but I do not deny the superiority of the 'virtuous' to the 'vicious' way of life' (pp. 192–3). You say I deny that the way things are comes 'from intelligence and design', but this does not change the way we should conduct our lives (p. 193). If you claim that belief in 'divine providence' leads to a greater expectation of 'reward of the good, and punishment of the bad', I again 'find the same fallacy': you still believe that, if 'divine existence' is granted, you may 'infer consequences from it', and add to the 'experienced order of nature', by arguing to them from 'the attributes which you ascribe to your gods' (p. 193). However, you cannot argue from 'causes to effects' (p. 193).

And what of the 'vain reasoners', who, instead of treating the 'present scene' as the 'sole object of their contemplation', regard 'this life' as just a **passage to something farther** (p. 193)? They get their 'idea of the gods' from their own 'imagination', for 'present phaenomena' point to nothing beyond themselves (p. 193). The 'divinity' may possess undiscovered 'attributes', but this is mere 'hypothesis' (p. 193). ATHENIANS, it is 'in vain' that our 'limited understanding' tries to go beyond the 'experienced train of events' (p. 194). When we 'argue from the course of nature', and infer an **intelligent cause** that gives it 'order', we embrace an 'uncertain and useless' principle: the subject is outside 'human experience', and, as knowledge of the cause comes 'entirely from the course of nature', we cannot return from this cause with 'any new inference' (p. 194).

As he had finished 'his harangue', I said that, by (rightly) making experience 'the only standard of our judgment' in 'questions of fact', he had provided a possible means of refuting Epicurus (p. 194). If you saw a 'half-finished building', why could you not '*infer* from the effect' that it was a 'work of design', and then go back from the 'inferred cause' to infer 'new additions' to it (p. 194)? If the world and this life are thought of as 'an imperfect building', from which a 'superior intelligence' can be inferred, why should it not then be argued that this 'intelligence' will 'leave nothing imperfect', allowing a 'more finished' plan of the world to be inferred (p. 195)? His reason was the 'infinite difference of the subjects' (p. 195). With human artefacts, we can move from 'the effect to the cause', and form 'new inferences' about the former, because our 'experience' of human beings is so extensive (p. 195). When we know something has been produced by human 'skill and industry', we can 'draw a hundred inferences' about it, based on 'experience and observation'; but this would not be possible, if we knew human beings from only one 'production' (p. 195). By itself, a footprint 'in the sand' only proves there was 'some figure' that 'produced' it, but a human footprint proves that there was 'probably another', which has been 'effaced' (p. 195). In 'this case', we apply numerous 'experiences and observations' of human beings and human behaviour (p. 195). But 'the **Deity**' is a 'single being in the universe', who does not belong to 'any species', from whose 'experienced attributes' we can infer his (p. 196). We cannot 'argue from the cause' (God), or infer any alteration in the effect (the universe), unless we actually observe it (p. 196). Every 'supposed addition to the works of nature' adds to its author's 'attributes', but, being 'entirely unsupported' by 'reason or argument', they are 'mere conjecture' (p. 196). Our error is to think of ourselves as 'the **Supreme Being**', and to believe he will act as we would 'in his situation' (p. 196). But it breaches 'all rules of analogy' to argue from human 'intentions' to those of 'a Being so different' (pp. 196–7). God has 'less analogy' to any other 'being in the universe' than 'the sun to a waxen paper'; from the 'faint traces' he discloses of himself, we cannot ascribe 'any attribute or perfection' to him (p. 197). Neither philosophy, nor religion, can take us 'beyond the usual course of experience', and no 'new fact', or expectation of 'reward or punishment', can be 'inferred from the religious hypothesis', beyond what is known from 'observation' (p. 197). Thus, he thought his '**apology** for EPICURUS' to be 'satisfactory' (p. 197).

I rejected his conclusion. He was saying that 'religious doctrines' have no 'influence on life', because they '*ought*' not to, but human beings do not 'reason' like this (p. 197). Their conduct is influenced by belief in God and the possibility of reward or punishment, and those who try to 'disabuse them' of this belief make it easier for them to break 'the laws of society' (p. 197). However, I agreed with his 'general conclusion in favour of liberty' (p. 197). States should 'tolerate' all philosophical ideas: refusing toleration paved the way for 'persecution and oppression' (p. 198). I doubted, though, that a cause could be 'known only by its effect', or have 'no parallel' with any other (p. 198). It would be hard to see how 'any conjecture' could be made about the 'cause' of an 'entirely singular' effect, which resembled nothing else (p. 198). If there is to be any role for 'experience' and 'analogy', both 'effect and cause' must have some 'resemblance' to others we know (p. 198). As Epicurus' opponents regard the universe,

68

a 'singular and unparalleled' effect, as 'proof of a Deity', his 'reasonings' about that deserved attention (p. 198). It was certainly hard to see how one could 'return from the cause to the effect' (p. 198).

Section 12
Of the Academical or Sceptical Philosophy (pp. 199–211)

Part 1 (pp. 199–203)

There are numerous 'philosophical' arguments for God's existence, but 'religious philosophers' still 'dispute' whether anyone could be so 'blinded' as to be an **'atheist'** (p. 199). The *'Sceptic'* is another 'enemy of religion', but what is 'a sceptic', and how far can we press 'doubt and uncertainty' (p. 199)? There is **Descartes'** *'antecedent'* scepticism, which advocates 'universal doubt' about all our 'opinions', 'principles' and even our 'faculties', to find an absolutely certain 'original principle' as a base for knowledge; but there is none (p. 199). So, **'CARTESIAN doubt'**, if attainable, would be 'entirely incurable' (p. 199). But a measure of this 'species of scepticism' assists philosophical enquiry, by ensuring 'impartiality' of judgement and freedom from 'prejudices' (p. 200). There is also *'consequent'* **scepticism**, which follows 'science and enquiry', and as part of which 'our very senses' may be 'brought into dispute' (p. 200). I am not referring here to the kind of 'trite' issues, which arise from the 'imperfection' of our sense organs, as when an oar has a 'crooked appearance' in water; these just show that we cannot depend on our 'senses alone', but must 'correct their evidence by reason' (p. 200). However, there are 'more profound arguments against the senses', which are less easily resolved (p. 200). 'Natural instinct' leads us to put 'faith' in them (p. 200). Without 'reasoning', we 'suppose' there is an **'external universe'**, which exists independently of 'our perception', and that the 'images, presented by the senses' (as of 'this very table') are 'external objects', the existence of which is unaffected by our 'presence' or 'absence' (pp. 200–1).

A little philosophy soon destroys this 'universal' opinion, by teaching us that what is 'present to the mind' is only an **'image** or perception': the table we see 'seems to diminish', as we move away from it, but the 'real table' does not change (p. 201). Thus, reason contradicts the 'primary instincts of nature', necessitating a 'new system' in relation to 'our senses'; but how can philosophy 'justify' it against the 'objections of the sceptics' (p. 201)? How (particularly when they appear 'in dreams') can it prove that the 'perceptions of the mind must be caused by external objects', which differ from, but resemble them, rather than being created by the mind itself or caused by 'some invisible and **unknown spirit'** (pp. 201–2)? Experience cannot decide the matter, because only the perceptions are 'present' to the mind, and there is no possibility of experiencing their 'connexion with objects', while falling back on 'the **veracity of the Supreme Being'** would be an 'unexpected' move (p. 202).

This is 'a topic' on which philosophical sceptics 'always triumph' (p. 202). They say that if we follow our natural instincts, we will believe the 'perception' to be the 'external object'; but that, if we treat perceptions as 'only representations of something external', we will abandon our natural instincts, fail to satisfy reason, and be unable to find a 'convincing argument' that connects our perceptions with 'external objects' (p. 202). Further, it is 'universally allowed' that all such **'sensible qualities'** as 'hard, soft, hot' do not exist in 'the objects', but are '**secondary**' perceptions 'of the mind' (p. 202). But, if so, this must apply to the 'supposed **primary qualities** of **extension and solidity**', which are 'acquired from the senses of sight and feeling': unless we hold they are obtained 'by *Abstraction*' (p. 203). But this is 'unintelligible': an extension that is 'neither tangible nor visible' is not conceivable (p. 203). Thus, one objection to the 'evidence of sense or to the opinion of external existence' is that, if it is based on 'natural instinct', it is 'contrary to reason', but if it is 'referred to reason', it is 'contrary to natural instinct' (p. 203). Another is that it is 'contrary to reason' that 'all sensible qualities are in the mind, not in the object'; if matter is stripped of its 'intelligible qualities', what remains is just an 'unknown, inexplicable *something*', which causes 'our perceptions' (p. 203).

Part 2 (pp. 204–7)

It may seem 'extravagant' for sceptics to try to 'destroy *reason* by argument', but this is their aim: they seek 'objections' to both 'abstract reasonings' and those about 'fact and existence' (p. 204). With the former, their main objection is the 'absurdity' of our '**ideas of space and time**' (p. 204). The '**infinite divisibility of extension**', for example, seems more shocking to 'common sense' than '**priestly** *dogmas*' (p. 204). Nothing could be 'more convincing and satisfactory' than our 'conclusions' about 'the properties of circles and triangles' and their implications, but even without the 'suggestions' of the sceptics, they throw reason into 'a kind of amazement' (pp. 204–5). She sees 'a full light', illuminating 'certain places', but it borders on 'profound darkness'; and the difficulties 'with regard to time' seem, 'if possible, still more palpable' (p. 205). However, reason must be 'restless and unquiet', even in relation to the 'scepticism, to which she is driven': nothing can be 'more sceptical, or more full of doubt and hesitation, than this scepticism itself' (p. 205).

Sceptical 'objections' to 'reasonings concerning matter of fact' are either '*popular* or *philosophical*' (pp. 205–6). The former arise from the limitations of 'human understanding', and relate to such things as the 'contradictory opinions', held in or by 'different ages', 'nations' and individuals (p. 206). They are weak, for in life, we reason all the time about 'fact and existence', and would not survive long if we did not (p. 206). 'Action' and the 'occupations of common life' are the best ways to drive out '**PYRRHONISM** or the excessive principles of scepticism' (p. 206). These may 'flourish' in the school or study, where it seems 'impossible, to refute them', but 'vanish like smoke' in the outside world, leaving even the 'most determined sceptic' in the 'same condition as other mortals' (p. 206).

The sceptic is on firmer ground with '*philosophical* objections' (p. 206). He can argue that, outside 'sense or memory', our only evidence for 'any matter of fact' is the 'relation of cause and effect'; that this derives from our seeing 'two objects' often '*conjoined* together'; that we have no basis, apart from 'custom' or 'instinct', for believing they will continue to be; and that custom or instinct, though 'difficult to resist', may deceive us (p. 206). However, the most powerful 'objection' to '*excessive* scepticism' is that 'no durable good' ever results from it (p. 206). A '**STOIC** or **EPICUREAN**' puts forward principles that may affect 'conduct and behaviour', but a 'PYRRHONIAN' cannot expect his philosophy to be, in any way, 'beneficial to society' (p. 207). Indeed, 'human life' would 'perish' if his principles prevailed: people would sink into 'total lethargy' (p. 207). But nature is 'too strong' (p. 207). A 'PYRRHONIAN' may astound 'himself or others' for a little while, but the 'most trivial event' will chase away his 'doubts and scruples', leaving him in the same state as everyone else (p. 207). He will have to admit that his objections merely highlight 'the **whimsical condition of mankind**', whose nature is to 'act and reason and believe', even though they cannot satisfy themselves as to 'the foundation of these operations' (p. 207).

Part 3 (pp. 207–11)

There is a '*mitigated* scepticism', or '**ACADEMICAL philosophy**', which is 'durable and useful' (p. 207). Human beings tend to be '**dogmatical** in their opinions', and to see only 'one side' of an argument (p. 207). A modest element 'of PYRRHONISM' could bring out the 'infirmities of human understanding', curb people's 'prejudice' against views that differ from their own, and (where it exists) 'abate' the 'pride' of 'the learned', by showing that the 'advantages' they have over others are 'inconsiderable, if compared with the universal complexity and confusion, which is inherent in human nature' (p. 208). Further, such limited scepticism might lead us to confine our 'enquiries' to subjects suited to 'the narrow capacity of human understanding' (p. 208). The human '*imagination*', bored with 'familiar' subjects, soars to 'whatever is remote and extraordinary', whereas we should concentrate on matters that relate to 'common life' and experience, where many matters need to be 'methodized and corrected' (p. 208). While we cannot explain why 'a stone will fall, or fire burn', we are unlikely to reach any satisfactory conclusions about 'the origin of worlds' (p. 209).

Examination of 'the natural powers of the human mind', show how appropriate it is to keep our enquiries within this 'narrow limitation' (p. 209). 'Quantity and number' are the only objects of 'the **abstract sciences**' or 'demonstration'; we can 'never advance further', and attempts to do so are 'mere **sophistry** and illusion' (p. 209). The 'undeterminate meaning of words' also causes confusion (p. 209). For example, to convince us of the truth of the statement, *'where there is no property, there can be no injustice'*, it is 'only necessary to define the terms' (p. 209). Other human enquiries concern 'only matter of fact and existence': 'whatever *is* may *not be*', so no 'negation of a fact' implies a contradiction (p. 209). Saying '**CAESAR**' never existed may be a 'false proposition', but it is 'perfectly conceivable, and implies no contradiction' (p. 210). However, that 'the cube root of 64 is equal to the half of 10' cannot be 'distinctly conceived' (p. 210). Thus, while *'a priori'* reasoning may 'produce any thing', any being's 'existence' can only be proved by 'arguments from its cause or its effect'; and it is only 'experience' that 'teaches us' the 'bounds of cause and effect', enabling us 'to infer the existence of one object from another', which is 'the source' of most 'human knowledge', 'action and behaviour' (p. 210). History and geography concern 'particular' facts, whereas the 'sciences' and 'politics' concern 'general' ones (p. 210). '**Theology**', proving God's existence and the 'immortality of souls', comprises both, and so, as 'supported by experience', has a basis in *'reason'*: but its 'solid foundation is *faith* and divine revelation' (p. 210). 'Morals and criticism' are objects of 'taste', rather than 'understanding' (p. 210).

Applying the above principles would cause 'havoc' in a library (p. 211). Of a volume of '**divinity**' or 'school metaphysics', we would ask: does *'it contain any abstract reasoning concerning quantity or number'*, or *'any experimental reasoning concerning matter of fact and existence'* (p. 211)? If not, it can be committed 'to the flames' as 'sophistry and illusion' (p. 211).

Overview

The following section is a chapter-by-chapter Overview of the 12 chapters in David Hume's *An Enquiry Concerning Human Understanding,* designed for quick reference to the Detailed Summary above. Readers may also find it particularly helpful for revision.

Section 1
Of the Different Species of Philosophy (pp. 87–95)

Hume explains there are two ways of approaching what he calls the science of human nature. One type of philosopher treats human beings as chiefly born for action, and tries to make people virtuous, by promoting sound principles of conduct, and emphasizing the difference between vice and virtue. The other sees human beings as primarily rational, and wants to develop their understanding by exploring the principles that govern human understanding and lead people to approve or disapprove of things. They feel that philosophy should have established the basis of morality by now. They work from particular instances to general principles, until they reach the original principles and the limits of what can be known.

The second kind may produce arguments that completely contradict popular opinion, so most people prefer the first, easy kind of philosophy, which relates more closely to ordinary life, and improves conduct. A philosopher who appeals to common sense is more likely to be honoured by future generations, which is why (Hume thinks) Cicero is more highly regarded than Aristotle, and Addison than Locke. Philosophers are not thought to contribute much of benefit to society, although ignorance is despised even more. The perfect character is thought to be equally at home with books, in company and in business, and to conduct his life by high ideals and wise principles. As human beings are intellectual, sociable and active beings, a varied life suits them best, so they should pursue knowledge in a way that relates it to activity and society: preoccupation with abstruse thought results in uncertainty and melancholy, while its discoveries are often coldly received. If it were just that people preferred easy philosophy, it might be right to let the matter pass, but they seem to reject any profound thinking, such as in metaphysics. Hume wonders if anything can be said in its defence.

He thinks abstract philosophy does benefit society. Even those who wish to write about, or paint, the outward appearances of life do so more successfully, if they know about human understanding and passions, and the feelings that distinguish vice from virtue. Anatomy seems disagreeable, but helps those wishing to paint a Venus or Helen, who need to know about the human body. People benefit from the spirit of accuracy that philosophy engenders, even though philosophers themselves may keep aloof from society. Further, science and learning are the most agreeable paths to follow in life: the research may be painful and tiring, but some minds thrive on the severe challenge, while bringing light from obscurity is always delightful.

It is said that abstract philosophy causes uncertainty and error, and that a lot of metaphysics arises from human beings trying to grasp what cannot be understood, or from popular superstitions. But this is why philosophers must persevere. Learning can only be freed from these abstruse questions by investigation of human understanding, and showing that its powers are unsuited to such subjects. Knowledge of human powers is important, as mental operations need to be distinguished from each other, put in order, and properly classified. Ignorance of the subject is contemptible in those professing to love learning, and such an investigation is within human capabilities. Reflection shows that the mind has several distinct powers, such as the will, understanding and imagination, and it is reasonable to hope that philosophy can discover what makes the human mind work, just as Newton did with the laws governing the revolutions of the planets. People should not be pessimistic about the prospects of success. Researching the human mind may be hard, but it will be profitable, if it increases knowledge.

Hume explains that his current enquiry is intended to throw light on matters, from which uncertainty and obscurity have deterred both the wise and the ignorant. He hopes to unite profound enquiry with clarity, truth and novelty, and remove the basis of an abstruse philosophy, which has sheltered superstition.

Section 2
Of the Origin of Ideas (pp. 96–100)

All recognize the difference between feeling the pain of too much heat, and remembering or imagining the sensation, which lacks the force of the original: the thought, however lively, is always inferior to the sensation, however dull. Similarly, actual anger is very different from thinking of it. Thus, mental perceptions divide into two classes: the less vivid thoughts and what might be called impressions, as of hearing, seeing, feeling and so on. Human thought seems able to surmount the limits of nature and reality, and to conceive things that have never been seen or heard: nothing is beyond its power, except what implies an absolute contradiction. But its actual limits are very narrow: its creative power is only one of combining information from the senses. Thus, a virtuous horse brings together virtue and a familiar animal. So, all ideas are copies of impressions or more lively ones. Even the idea of God, as an infinitely wise and good being, derives from reflection on human mental operations, and thinking of the qualities of goodness and wisdom as unlimited. Those who disagree should try to produce an idea not derived from this source.

If a defect makes someone incapable of a particular kind of sensation, he will not possess the corresponding idea. A blind person can form no idea of colours, and the same is true of the passions: a selfish person has little idea of generosity. This could dispel a lot of metaphysical jargon. All ideas, particularly abstract ones, are faint, and liable to be confused with others, which resemble them, so when a term is used often, we tend to think there is a definite idea attached to it, even if it has no distinct meaning. But impressions are vivid, and harder to make mistakes about. Thus, if we use a philosophical term that has no meaning, we must check there is an impression from which the idea came. Bringing ideas into a clear light, in this way, should help to end disputes about their nature and reality.

Section 3
Of the Association of Ideas (pp. 101–7)

A principle of connection exists between the mind's different thoughts and ideas, so that they present themselves to the memory or imagination in a regular way; but no philosopher has tried to classify the principles of association. There seem to be three: resemblance, contiguity in time or place, and cause and effect. For example, in narrative compositions, the events must be related to each other in the imagination, and form a unity. A historian of Europe would be influenced by contiguity of space and period of time: all the events he wrote about would have unity in this respect. The most common type of connection is cause and effect, and the historian knows its importance, since it enables us to control events, and influence the future.

This gives some idea of unity of action, which is needed in all literary works. Both a biographer of Achilles and a poet, writing about him, would link events by showing their mutual dependence and relationship. A person's actions depend on each other, not only during a short period of his life, but throughout it, so removing one link would affect the whole series of events. This connection is particularly close in epic poetry, because it takes its readers nearer to the people and events it deals with than, for example, history or biography. If a poet covers too long a period of time, too many events, or moves away from the central characters or the centre of action, his readers' interest flags. Unity is also required in history, in which events are connected by the relation of cause and effect, although the connections are not as close as in epic poetry. Thus, while the whole Peloponnesian War is a suitable historical subject, the siege of Athens alone is more appropriate for an epic poem. Homer manages to achieve sufficient unity in his treatment of Achilles and Hector, as does Milton, in *Paradise Lost*.

All this suggests that many mental operations depend on the association of ideas. The sympathy between the passions and imagination is particularly noteworthy, and it can be seen that the affections aroused by one object pass easily into another, connected one, but not into unconnected ones. Although this principle cannot be investigated exhaustively here, it is enough to have established that the three principles connecting all ideas are resemblance, contiguity and causation.

Section 4
Sceptical Doubts Concerning the Operations of the Understanding (pp. 108–18)

Part 1 (pp. 108–13)

All objects of human reason or enquiry divide into relations of ideas and matters of fact. The first includes all propositions that are demonstratively certain, such as those of geometry and arithmetic: for example, 'three times five is equal to half of thirty'. Their truth is discovered by thought alone, and does not depend on what exists in the world. Matters of fact are very different, as their denial does not involve a contradiction. For example, the proposition 'the sun will not rise tomorrow' is intelligible, and its falsehood cannot be demonstrated logically. This raises the question of what evidence there is for matters of fact beyond the testimony of the senses and memory. Hume thinks this is a neglected area of philosophy.

Reasoning about matters of fact seems to be based on the relation of cause and effect, which enables human beings to go beyond memory and the senses. Thus, someone finding a watch on a desert island would conclude that people had been there. Analysis of other reasonings of this type shows they are also based on cause and effect. Heat and light, for example, are collateral effects of fire, and one may be inferred from the other. Knowledge of cause and effect is not obtained by *a priori* reasonings, but comes from experience of the constant conjunction of particular objects. However, no object shows, through the qualities apparent to the senses, either the causes that produced it, or the effects it will produce; so reason, unassisted by experience, cannot draw any inferences about real existence and matters of fact. That causes and effects can only be discovered through experience is confirmed by the fact that, prior to familiarity with particular objects, there is no way of predicting their effects: for example, gunpowder's explosive qualities could not be discovered by *a priori* reasoning. However, we tend to think this does not apply to events that have been familiar from birth. So great is the influence of custom that people think they have always known that one billiard ball communicates motion to another on impact.

But there is no way of knowing an object's effect, except from past observation. For example, motion in the second billiard ball is wholly distinct from that in the first, so without experience, it might be thought that any effect (such as its returning in a straight line) could result from the impact of the first. An attempt to determine any single event, or infer any cause or effect, without using observation and experience, would be pointless.

This is why no sensible philosopher tries to determine the ultimate cause of any natural process. The most that human beings can do, by using experience and observation, is to group as many particular effects as possible under a few general causes; but the causes of these will never be discovered. This suggests that philosophical enquiry only serves to highlight our ignorance. Applying geometry to scientific problems does not lead to knowledge of ultimate causes, as its use is based on the assumption that there are natural laws. It may help with the application of such laws, but their discovery is due to experience. Abstract reasoning about an object cannot suggest its effect, or indicate the inseparable connection between cause and effect.

Part 2 (pp. 113–18)

As all reasoning about matters of fact seems to be based on the relation of cause and effect, while all conclusions about it are drawn from experience, Hume reflects on the basis of conclusions drawn from experience. They are not based on reasoning, or any process of the understanding, and nature does not disclose its secrets to human beings. For example, the senses give information about the colour, weight, and consistency of bread, but neither they nor reason can tell how it nourishes the body. However, though ignorant of natural powers and principles, human beings take it that, when they see similar qualities in things, they will have similar powers, and so expect them to produce effects similar to those already observed.

Past experience gives direct and certain information about particular things, at a particular time, so why is this extended to other things and the future? It is because an inference is made. The propositions, 'I have found that a particular object always has a certain effect'; and, 'I foresee that other, similar objects will have similar effects', are not the same; but the second is always inferred from the first. Hume asks what the connecting proposition, or intermediate step, is. Reasoning can be divided into two kinds: demonstrative reasoning about the relation of ideas, and reasoning about matters of fact and existence. The first kind does not apply, as no contradiction is involved in holding that an object, similar to those experienced, may produce different effects. It is not contradictory to state, for example, that trees will grow leaves in January, and lose them in May. Therefore, the second group is the relevant one. But the argument that past experience should be trusted is only probable. Arguments about existence and matters of fact are based on cause and effect; knowledge of this derives from experience; and all the conclusions drawn presuppose that the future will conform to the past. Thus, all arguments from experience are based on the similarity of natural objects, such that apparently similar causes are expected to produce similar effects. It is only after a long series of uniform experiences of it that human beings feel they can be certain about a particular event.

Hume wonders how experience, merely by showing a number of uniform effects from certain objects, removes ignorance about the powers of all objects? Similar effects are expected from similar objects, but this step needs to be explained. It is not intuitive or demonstrative, and it begs the question to call it experimental, as all inferences from experience assume that the future will resemble the past. As experience would be useless, if nature were to change, arguments from experience cannot prove the resemblance of past to future, as they are based on it. That things happen in a predictable way now does not prove they will do so in future. This raises the question of why human beings never think they will not always happen in the same way: which is what enables even stupid people to learn from experience. What Hume wants to stress is that it is not a process of reasoning that leads people to expect the past to resemble the future, or apparently similar causes to produce similar effects.

Section 5
Sceptical Solution of these Doubts (pp. 119–30)

Part 1 (pp. 119–24)

Although it aims at eliminating vices, love of philosophy can result in people reasoning themselves out of virtue: focusing on the vanity of life may just be a way of justifying natural idleness. But this does not apply to (moderately) sceptical philosophy, which discourages hasty judgements and philosophical speculation outside the limits of ordinary life. Hume thinks it surprising that it is criticized so much: although its very opposition to so many vices may create enemies. Such moderate scepticism will not raise doubts that will destroy all action. While it is true that, in reasoning from experience, the mind does take a step, which is unsupported by any argument, there is no danger that moderate scepticism will affect this step, on which all knowledge depends. While human nature remains the same, whatever principle leads human beings to make it will go on exerting its influence. An intelligent newcomer to the world would observe a continual succession of objects, but would not immediately discover the idea of cause and effect, as it is not reasonable to suppose that, just because one event precedes another, it is its cause. Without more experience, he would be unable to reason about any matter of fact, not immediately present to his memory or senses. But, after a while, through observing the constant conjunction of certain events, he would infer their causal relationship, even though he still would not know how one produces the other. It is the principle of custom that would lead him to do so. Although we do not know the ultimate reason why a particular act is repeated, custom is the ultimate principle of human nature, in relation to all conclusions from experience. All inferences from experience are the result of custom (the great guide in life), not reasoning. Without it, nothing would be known beyond what is immediately present to the memory and senses.

Although conclusions from experience take us beyond memory and the senses, some fact must be present to them, to lead us to do so. What this means is that all beliefs about matters of fact or real existence are derived from some object, present to the senses, and a customary connection between it and another object. Having found, for example, that flame and heat are always connected, when flame is present to the senses, custom leads the mind to expect heat. No thought process could produce natural instincts of this type. Philosophical investigation could stop here, as it is impossible to go further. But there is an understandable desire to examine the nature of this belief and the customary connection, from which it derives, more closely.

Part 2 (pp. 124–30)

The human imagination cannot exceed the stock of ideas it receives from the senses, but has an unlimited power of combining them. As no matter of fact is so firmly believed that the contrary cannot be conceived, the difference between fiction and belief is the feeling associated with the latter. This feeling is belief, which is a more lively conception of an object than the imagination can achieve. The imagination can mix and vary its ideas, but never reaches belief, which distinguishes the ideas of the judgement from the fictions of the imagination, making them the ruling principle of our actions; and, if belief is just a more intense and steady state of mind than that accompanying the fictions of the imagination, and which arises from the customary conjunction of an object with something present to our senses, it should not be hard to find other similar mental operations.

The principles of connection, uniting our thoughts, have been reduced to resemblance, contiguity and causation. When an object is present to sense or memory, the mind seems to be drawn to the idea of the related object, and also achieves a firmer conception of it. This certainly is the case with cause and effect, suggesting a general law of mental operations. Roman Catholics, for example, claim that their rituals and images enliven their devotion, suggesting that the effect of resemblance in enlivening ideas is common. With contiguity, the presence of an object takes the mind to it with greater liveliness, and the same is true of causation. Of course, belief in the correlative object is always assumed: being close to home cannot excite our ideas of it, unless we believe it exists. When belief goes beyond the memory or senses, it derives from similar causes. Dry wood being thrown on the fire immediately makes the mind think it will add to, not diminish, the flame. This movement of thought from cause to effect does not come from reason, but from custom and experience; and, as it starts with an object present to the senses, it makes the idea of flame livelier than it could be in the imagination. And what causes such a strong conception is the presence of an object and being accustomed to move to the idea of another. This is how the mind works in relation to conclusions about matters of fact and existence.

There is a pre-established harmony, based on custom, between the course of nature and the succession of our ideas: without it, knowledge would be limited to memory and the senses. This mental operation, of inferring like effects from like causes, could not be performed by reason, which is error-prone, and only develops after infancy. It has to be a mechanical operation, implanted in us by nature, which starts at birth.

Section 6
Of Probability (pp. 131–3)

There may be no such thing as chance, but ignorance of the real cause of events leads to a similar type of belief: probability arises from there being a greater chance of one outcome than another. When a dice is thrown, it is thought equally probable that any side will turn up, this being the nature of chance. But, if a dice is marked with one number on four sides, and a different one on two, it is more probable that the first will turn up, and that is the one expected to turn up more frequently. This imprints the idea more strongly on the imagination, leading to that security of expectation, which constitutes the nature of belief.

The same is true of the probability of causes. Some causes, such as the law of gravity, are uniform, and show no irregularity, while others are uncertain in their effects. But when a cause does not produce its usual effect, this is attributed, not to an irregularity in nature, but to the presence of an unknown cause. In all our inferences, we transfer past to future, and, where the former has been entirely regular, always expect the event to occur. But where causes, apparently exactly similar, have been found to produce different effects, we take account of this when determining the probability of the event, expecting the event that has occurred most often.

Section 7
Of the Idea of Necessary Connexion (pp. 134–47)

Part 1 (pp. 134–43)

Hume notes that lack of progress in the moral sciences suggests they require great care. In metaphysics, no ideas are more obscure and uncertain than 'power', 'force', 'energy' and 'necessary connection'. He wants to establish their exact meaning. He has explained above that ideas are copies of impressions. Complex ideas can be known by definition, but this just enumerates the simple ideas of which they consist. But, as these may be ambiguous, the impressions, from which the ideas are copied, must be produced, to throw light on them. To be fully acquainted with necessary connection, its impression must be examined in the sources from which it derives.

If our minds could discover the power of any cause, it would be possible to foresee its effect. But there is no inward impression of a necessary connection between cause and effect; it is just apparent, to the outer senses, that one follows the other. In the universe, things follow each another (heat, for example, always accompanies flame) in uninterrupted succession, but human beings do not know what connects them. However, they are aware of the internal power, by which the will exercises control over the bodily organs and the faculties of the soul, so perhaps the idea of necessary connection can be derived from reflection on the operations of the mind. But, despite the constant awareness that bodily motion follows volition, it is impossible to discover how the will carries out this operation. Nothing in nature is more mysterious than the union of body and soul, which gives a spiritual substance influence over a material one. It is not even known why human beings can move some bodily organs, like the fingers, but not others. The will's influence is learned from experience alone, which shows one event following another, but not how they are connected. Anatomy shows that the immediate object in voluntary motion is not the part of the body itself, but muscles and nerves, underlining the mysterious nature of the power by which we move our limbs, which we cannot understand.

Hume wonders if there is consciousness of a power in the mind, when, by an act of will, we bring to it, and contemplate, a new idea. He thinks not. To know a power, it must be known how a particular cause produces its effect. However, we do not know the nature of the human soul, that of an idea, or how one produces the other. We just experience the event. Further, the mind's command over itself is limited, and knowledge of these limits comes from experience, not reason. Again, self-command is greater at some times than others, but there seems to be no reason for these variations. So far from understanding the energy of the will, experience is essential to convince us that such effects can be produced by a simple act of volition.

Most people can explain familiar natural processes: through long habit, they expect the effect when the cause appears. But when extraordinary events, like earthquakes, occur, they cannot find a cause in the ordinary powers of nature, and fall back on some unseen cause. Philosophers, on the other hand, recognize that the cause of even familiar events is unknown. Some of them argue that the actual cause of every effect is to be found, not in nature, but in God's will: he wills the constant conjunction of certain objects, according to the general laws of the universe he has laid down. And, as we do not understand how mind affects body, they also assert that God causes the union of soul and body, and that divine volition, not our senses, produces sensations of external objects in the mind and movement in the limbs. Some even say that God reveals our ideas to us. They think this makes God seem more powerful, but it would suggest more power in God that he should have been able to create a world, which, by its normal operation, fulfils all his purposes, than that he should have to intervene continually to adjust its parts. Anyway, such a theory takes us beyond experience and outside the scope of our faculties. We do not know how the supreme mind operates, and have no idea of God, except through reflection on our own faculties.

Part 2 (pp. 143–7)

It is pointless to search for an idea of necessary connection: there is only one event following another. All events seem conjoined, but not connected. But, although observing one event following another does not entitle us to form a general rule, when a whole species of event has always been conjoined with another, they are always called cause and effect. Thus, it is from habit, and the connection felt in the mind, that the idea of necessary connection is formed. Saying two objects are connected means they are connected in thought. This shows the weakness of the understanding. Although all human reasoning about fact and existence is based on cause and effect, it is impossible to give a satisfactory definition of a cause. On the basis of experience, a cause can only be defined as: one object, followed by another, where all the objects, similar to the first, are followed by objects similar to the second; or: one object followed by another, the appearance of which always conveys the thought to that other. Nothing produces any impression, or suggests any idea, of necessary connection; but many uniform instances of the same event following the same object indicate cause, and produce a customary connection in thought between an object and what usually accompanies it.

Section 8
Of Liberty and Necessity (pp. 148–164)

Part 1 (pp. 148–59)

Hume observes that exact definition of terms might be expected in issues that have been discussed for many years. However, ambiguity in the terms, and disputants attaching different ideas to them, may have prolonged a controversy. This is the case with the question of liberty and necessity, where both educated and ignorant people probably share the same opinion, and a few clear definitions would resolve the issue. All accept that the laws of nature determine the degree and direction of every motion. If nature were always changing, so that no two events were like each other, there could be no concept of necessity and causation, which arise from uniformity in natural processes. Human beings get the idea of necessity and causation from the constant conjunction of similar objects, and the inference from one to another. If they have always accepted that these apply to voluntary human actions, it follows they have always accepted the doctrine of necessity, and any dispute results from misunderstanding.

It is generally agreed that human nature is the same down the ages. Such motives as ambition and avarice always produce the same actions. The wars, intrigues and revolutions of history, together with our experience of other people, enable us to discover the universal principles of human nature; and without such uniformity in human actions, experience would serve no purpose. Of course, allowance must be made for diversity of character and opinion: absolute uniformity is not found in any part of nature. Differences also exist between countries, the sexes, and different generations. Again, not all causes are linked to their usual effects with the same uniformity. While ordinary people always attribute the uncertainty of events to uncertainty in the causes, philosophers realize that all causes and effects are connected with equal necessity, so apparent uncertainty results from hidden causes. A peasant thinks a clock keeps stopping, because it does not go right, but a clock expert sees that, although the mechanism still operates in the same way, a grain of dust is jamming it. Similarly, philosophers and physicians know that the human body is a complicated machine, with many hidden powers, so apparently irregular events do not prove that the laws of nature are not operating in a regular way.

Thus, those who know every detail of character and situation may be able to explain human beings' apparently unexpected decisions. For example, a usually obliging person may be irritable from toothache. Despite apparent aberrations, human motives operate uniformly, and the regular conjunction between motives and voluntary actions is universally accepted, enabling us to make inferences about human actions. As society becomes more complex, the range of these actions may increase, but, on the basis of past experience, people, as well as objects, are expected to go on behaving in the same way; and all people, including philosophers, accept the doctrine of necessity. There could be no political science, if laws and forms of government did not influence society uniformly, while it is no more likely that a rich and honest person will enter his friend's house, and rob him, than that the latter's house will fall down.

However, people are reluctant to acknowledge the doctrine of necessity openly. They observe the constant conjunction of external objects, and accept necessary connection between cause and effect in relation to them. But, when they reflect on their own minds, they do not feel there is the same connection between motive and action, and think that effects, brought about by thought, are different from those resulting from material force. But once it is seen that constant conjunction also applies to voluntary actions, it is possible to accept that they have the necessity common to all causes. Ascribing necessity to the determinations of the will may be contrary to certain philosophical views, but any dissent is verbal, not substantial. The error is made of thinking that, with external objects, there is some further idea of necessity and causation that is not present in voluntary mental actions. It may be unattractive to set such narrow limits to human understanding, but we do apply necessity and causation to human beings, as we always draw inferences between human actions and motives.

So, reconciling liberty and necessity is a purely verbal question. Actions are undeniably connected with motives, and one follows uniformly from the other. 'Liberty' refers to the power of acting, or not acting, according to the determination of the will. Apart from a prisoner in chains, everyone possesses such liberty, which must be defined in a way that is consistent with the facts and with itself. Nothing exists without a cause, which cannot be defined without its including necessary connection with its effect. Unless objects were regularly conjoined with each other, there would be no concept of cause and effect. If this definition is accepted, there can be no such thing as liberty, as opposed to necessity, not constraint.

Hume warns that no more unacceptable form of philosophical reasoning exists than trying to refute a hypothesis, by claiming that it will harm religion or morality. Further, the doctrines of liberty and necessity, as well as being consistent with morality, are essential to it. 'Cause' can be defined in two ways: the constant conjunction of similar objects; or the inference, made by the understanding, from one object to another. Necessity, in both senses, has been universally regarded as belonging to the human will, and no one has tried to deny our ability to make inferences about human actions, or that these are based on experience of the conjunction of similar actions with similar motives. This is a harmless doctrine, with no implications for morality or religion. Laws are based on reward and punishment, which influence the mind, to produce good actions, and prevent evil ones; and this is an example of the necessity he is trying to establish. Unless actions result from some cause in the human character and disposition, people cannot be praised or blamed for what they do, even if they break all moral and religious rules. Without causes and necessity, a person could commit the most terrible crime, and still be blameless. We do not blame people for actions they perform in ignorance, but condemn them for bad actions that follow deliberation, because these prove criminal principles. The same arguments prove that liberty is also essential to morality, as we cannot hold people accountable for things they do as a result of constraint.

It may be argued that, if necessity applies to voluntary actions, there must be a chain of necessary causes, such that God has predetermined every human volition, and either humans are not responsible for their actions or they are God's fault. An infinitely wise and powerful being must have foreseen and intended all the human actions we call criminal, so either they are not criminal, as God has ordained them, or, if they are criminal, as God is responsible for them, we cannot ascribe perfection to him. Both views are absurd, irreverent and untrue. Some philosophers have contended that the world is ordered with perfect benevolence, and that every apparent physical evil is actually good. However, this will not convince those in pain. As for moral evils, nature has so formed human beings that they instinctively approve or condemn certain kinds of character or action, approving those that contribute to society's peace and security, and condemning those that harm it; and philosophical speculation is not going to persuade people to change their view of vice and virtue. As for God, it is hard to see how he could be the cause of all human actions, without being the author of sin; but reconciling apparently contingent human actions with divine prescience is beyond philosophy's power. It is better to confine enquiry to common life than embark on a sea of doubt, uncertainty and contradiction.

Section 9
Of the Reason of Animals (pp. 165–8)

Reasoning about matters of fact is based on the expectation that a cause will produce the same effects as similar ones. Where objects are entirely similar, the inference drawn is conclusive, but where the resemblance is less close, it has less force. Anatomical observations, made in relation to one type of animal, are extended to others; and the theory, put forward above, about how human understanding and passions operate, will be strengthened, if it explains similar phenomena in animals. They also learn from experience, and conclude that the same causes will produce the same results. They can be taught to do things, including those contrary to their natural instincts, by use of rewards and punishments.

Animal inferences cannot be based on reasoning, as they lack this ability, so nature must have provided some other means to enable them to infer effects from causes; and this is custom. However, although they acquire knowledge from observation, they also derive it from nature itself. This is instinct, and the experimental reasoning, which human beings share with animals, is a type of instinct, the operation of which is not governed by the intellect. Instinct teaches human beings to avoid fire, just as it teaches birds the art of incubation.

Section 10
Of Miracles (pp. 169–86)

Part 1 (pp. 169–73)

The authority of the Bible and Christian tradition is based on the testimony of the apostles, who witnessed Jesus' miracles. This makes the evidence for Christianity less than that for the truth of our senses, as it was no greater, and no one should be as confident in others' testimony as in things he sees himself. Thus, except where reinforced by the Holy Spirit, the evidence of scriptural revelation is less powerful than that of sense experience, which it contradicts. This provides a powerful argument against all kinds of superstitious delusion, such as miracles. Experience is the only guide in matters of fact, but as not all effects follow with equal certainty from their supposed causes, it is prone to error. While some events invariably follow one another, the conjunction of others is more variable, so the wise person proportions his belief to the evidence. In some cases, on the basis of past experience, he expects an event with complete certainty, but in others, he has to weigh conflicting evidence, and then reach a judgement on the basis of probability.

No type of reasoning is more useful than that based on eye-witness reports. However, it is only because experience shows that people tend to tell the truth that there is any confidence in human testimony. Whether evidence from it is regarded as proof or probability depends on the degree to which experience shows particular reports to be accurate. Experience and observation must always be the ultimate test, and there may be reason to doubt particular testimony, as when witnesses contradict each other, are of doubtful character, or have a vested interest in what they report. If the testimony is trying to establish something extraordinary, its force is proportionately reduced the more unusual it is. Witnesses and historians are believed, not because of any *a priori* connection between their testimony and reality, but because experience shows conformity between them. But when the fact attested is one that is seldom observed, experience itself, which generally leads to witnesses' testimony being trusted, causes it to be doubted.

The probability against the testimony of witnesses is increased, if what they claim is not only marvellous, but miraculous. A miracle is a violation of the laws of nature, and, as these have been established by invariable experience, they are the most powerful proofs against a miracle. The reason why it is more than probable that human beings will die, or that fire will consume wood, is that these events conform to the laws of nature, and it would need a miracle to prevent them. The term 'miracle' is not used of things that happen in the ordinary course of nature, so uniform experience is against miracles. Thus, no testimony is enough to establish a miracle, unless its not being true would be more miraculous than the miracle itself. If someone claims to have seen a dead man restored to life, it must be asked whether it is more probable that the event should have happened, or that the witness should deceive or be deceived, and the greater miracle rejected. The miracle would only be convincing if the falsehood of the testimony were more miraculous than the event described.

Part 2 (pp. 174–86)

There is no miracle in history, attested by sufficient people of undoubted integrity to prove they were not deluded, or intending to deceive. There is an element in human nature, which reduces any credit we should give to testimony about miracles. Generally, we work on the basis that what is most usual is more probable, and, where accounts of an event differ, use past observation to decide what happened. But, with an alleged miracle, there is a tendency to believe it, due to the agreeable nature of the surprise and wonder associated with it. And, if religion joins with love of wonder, common sense is thrown aside. All the bogus miracles that have been proved to be so prove human beings' inclination to believe the marvellous. We delight in passing on an interesting piece of news, and the same desire inclines us to believe and report miracles with complete conviction.

It is a strong presumption against accounts of miracles that they occur in uncivilized countries, or have been passed down from ignorant ancestors. The early history of all nations shows a very different attitude towards nature from that of today. Battles and famines never have natural causes, but are associated with omens and oracles. As Lucian recounts, the false prophet, Alexander, was wise to tell his tales first to the ignorant Pamphlagonians. He was able to gain a large following, and even attract the attention of Emperor Marcus Aurelius. Civilized and educated people are far less likely to believe such claims. Had Alexander been based in Athens, its philosophers would soon have used their reason and eloquence to open people's eyes. There are numerous witnesses against even alleged miracles that have not been proved false. In religious matters, what is different is contrary, so the different religions of, for example, Rome and Turkey cannot all have a solid foundation. A miracle claimed by one of them indirectly contradicts the alleged miracles of the others. When people recount a miracle in their particular religion, we should treat the account as if it referred to one in another religion, and expressly contradicted it. Cardinal de Retz records how many witnesses claimed that the cathedral doorkeeper at Saragossa recovered his lost leg, by rubbing holy oil on the stump. He gave no credit to the miracle, and did not think it necessary to try to disprove it, as it was self-evidently false. Miracles may be widely attested, but against them can be set their absolute impossibility, which all reasonable people will consider sufficient refutation.

Human testimony has great authority in some cases, but not in all. It is tempting to appear as a prophet from heaven, while the masses are always eager to accept wonderful stories uncritically. But when reports of miracles fly about, they must be treated as instances of credulity and delusion, not evidence of breaches of the laws of nature. Only experience can give authority to human testimony, but it confirms the laws of nature, so no testimony can prove a miracle, or establish it as the basis for any religious system. It is important to understand what is meant by a miracle. If every author agreed that, on 1 January 1600, the earth was in total darkness for eight days, this should not be doubted; rather, the causes should be investigated. But, if all historians stated that Queen Elizabeth died on 1 January 1600, but then returned to life, and governed England for three more years, this miraculous event could not be believed. However powerful the evidence, it would be too great a breach of the laws of nature.

Through the ages, people have been imposed upon by ridiculous stories of miracles, but, even if a miracle is ascribed to God, that does not make it any more probable, as God's attributes are unknown, except for human experience of his work in the order of nature. We must compare the lies people tell with the breaches of natural laws that it is claimed have occurred in alleged miracles, and judge which is more probable. This is why Bacon urged people to examine every claim about something extraordinary in nature, particularly if it is linked to religion, as those who recount such things have a strong appetite for falsehood. This is a better way of defending Christianity, which is based on faith, than human reason. The miracles in the Bible should be treated as the work of human writers, which appear in a book, full of extraordinary events, produced by an ignorant people, whose view of the world and human nature is very different from ours. Such a book's falsehood does not seem more miraculous than the miracles it relates, but it would have to be to meet the standard of probability, established above. Our conclusion must be that Christianity was not only attended by miracles, at the outset, but cannot be believed by a reasonable person today without one. Reason is insufficient to convince people of its truth, but whoever is moved by faith to accept it is aware of a continued miracle in his own person, which enables him to believe what is contrary to custom and experience.

Section 11
Of a Particular Providence and a Future State (pp. 187–98)

Hume describes how, in conversation with a friend, he had pointed out philosophy's good fortune in having begun in an age and country, where, unlike the present, it was given the freedom it needs. Protagoras may have been banished, and Socrates executed, but even Epicurus was allowed to live in Athens, while the Roman emperors gave financial support to all types of philosophers. But his friend had argued that the bigotry he thought fatal to philosophy actually sprang from it, as speculative religious ideas could not be conceived in an illiterate society. This bigotry had then joined with super stition, and turned against philosophy. In ancient times, harmonious relations had followed initial clashes between philosophy and established religion, with the former attracting the educated and the latter the masses. Hume had contended that this argument omitted politics, as society's rulers might try to suppress philosophical views, like those of Epicurus, because his denial of God's existence and a future life might undermine morality. His friend's view was that persecution always resulted from prejudice, not the perceived ill effects of particular philosophical ideas. He thought that Epicurus could have successfully defended his ideas to the Athenian public, so Hume had asked him to do so.

As Epicurus, his friend had argued that he did not wish to debate the origin of the world, or how it was governed, but to establish whether discussing such questions harmed the public interest. He hoped his audience would agree to allow him to pursue his enquiries. Present-day religious philoso phers, not content with traditional religious beliefs, which he accepted, wanted to base religion on reason. Pointing to the order, beauty, and apparent design of the universe, they asked if mere chance could have produced it. He did not challenge this argument, but held that such an approach proved the issue to be a speculative one, and that, when he denied the existence of God and a future state, he was not undermining society, but putting forward views his opponents, if they argued consistently, would have to accept.

They contended that the evidence of design in nature was the main argument for God's existence. Thus, they argued from effects to causes, inferring the forethought of the workman from the order of the work. But when a cause was inferred from an effect, only the qualities, sufficient to produce the effect, could be ascribed to the cause. It was not legitimate to ascribe further qualities to the inferred cause, or to infer from it other effects, beyond those by which alone it was known. If the gods were responsible for the universe's existence or order, they had exactly the degree of power, intelligence and goodness that appeared in their work. It was not possible to argue from the universe, the effect, to Jupiter, the cause, and then infer other effects from that cause.

He wanted to know on what basis philosophers claimed that their gods had any perfection not found in the universe. If they claimed to be drawing inferences from effects to causes, they had changed their argument, and were actually arguing from causes to effects, presuming that a more perfect world than the present one was better suited to their perfect gods. They argued that matter, or the laws of nature, limited Jupiter's power and goodness, causing him to create a world containing evil and disorder and thus unhappy humans. But they had no reason to assume that Jupiter was powerful or benevolent. The religious hypothesis was just one way of accounting for what was found in the universe. Those, who thought the apparent design of the universe proved a divine cause, were entitled to infer its existence; but, if they then argued from this inferred cause to the existence of something else in nature, which would provide a fuller display of God's attributes, they departed from their method of reasoning. They could not add to the effect, to make it more worthy of the cause.

He was accused of undermining morality, and denying God's existence, but he did not deny the superiority of a good to a wicked way of life, nor did his views affect conduct. His opponents claimed that belief in God meant greater expectation of the good being rewarded and the bad punished. But this committed the same fallacy of inferring consequences from God's existence, and adding to the experienced order of nature, by arguing to such additions from the attributes they ascribed to the gods.

There were those who regarded this life as just a passage to a future one. They got their idea of the gods from their imagination, for natural phenomena pointed to nothing beyond themselves. God might have undiscovered attributes, but this was mere speculation. Limited human understanding could not go beyond experience. Those who argued from the course of nature, and inferred an intelligent cause that gave it order, embraced a useless idea. The subject was outside human experience and, as knowledge of the cause came entirely from nature itself, they could not return from this cause with any new inference.

When he had finished, Hume commented that, while his friend was right to make experience the sole criterion in questions of fact, this gave a possible means of refuting Epicurus. If someone saw a half-finished building, it seemed legitimate to infer from this effect that it was a work of design, and then return from the inferred cause, to infer new additions to it. If the world and life were thought of as an unfinished building, from which a superior being could be inferred, it seemed reasonable to argue that this being would not leave it unfinished, allowing an idea of a more finished world to be formed. His friend had dismissed this on the grounds of the infinite difference between the subjects. With human artefacts, it was possible to move from effect to cause, and then form new inferences about the effect, as we have so much experience of human beings and what they produce; but this would not be possible, if our knowledge of human beings were limited to only one artefact. There was only one God in the universe, so he did not belong to any species, from experience of whose attributes we could infer his. We were not entitled to argue from the cause (God), or to infer any alteration in the effect (the universe), unless we actually observed it. Our mistake was to think of ourselves as God, and to believe he would act as we would in the same situation. But it breached all the rules of analogy to argue from human intentions to those of God, who bore no resemblance to other beings in the universe. From the faint traces he revealed of himself, it was not possible to ascribe any perfection to him. Neither philosophy, nor religion, could take human beings beyond the usual course of experience, and no new fact, or expectation of reward or punishment, could be inferred from the religious hypothesis, beyond what was known from observation.

Hume had rejected his conclusion. His friend was saying that religious beliefs did not influence life, because they should not do so, but this was not how the human mind worked. Belief in God, and the possibility of reward or punishment, did affect conduct, and those who questioned this belief make it easier for people to break the law. But he had agreed with his friend's general defence of liberty. States should tolerate all philosophical ideas. The alternative was persecution and oppression. He doubted that a cause could be known only by its effect, or could have no parallel with any other, as it would be hard to see how there could be any conjecture about the cause of a unique effect. For there to be any role for experience and analogy, both effect and cause had to resemble others we knew. But it was hard to see how one could return from the cause to the effect.

Section 12
Of the Academical or Sceptical Philosophy (pp. 199–211)

Part 1 (pp. 199–203)

Hume considers the nature of scepticism. Descartes had advocated universal doubt, to find an absolutely certain basis for knowledge, but there was none. So, if Cartesian doubt had been attainable, it would have been incurable. But a modicum of this type of scepticism assists philosophical enquiry, by ensuring impartial judgement and freedom from prejudice. There is a kind scepticism that questions the senses themselves. This is not the kind that arises from imperfections in the sense organs, as when an oar looks crooked in water: it goes much deeper. Natural instinct makes human beings put faith in their senses, so they believe there is an external universe, which exists independently of their perception, and that the images, presented by the senses, are external objects, the existence of which is unaffected by their presence or absence. Philosophy soon undermines this universal opinion, by teaching that what is present to the mind is only an image or perception: a table seems to get smaller, as we move away from it, but the real table does not change. Thus, reason contradicts natural instinct, and it is hard to see how philosophy can prove that mental perceptions are caused by external objects, which differ from, but resemble them, rather than being created by the mind itself, or caused by an invisible spirit. Experience cannot decide the matter, because only the perceptions are present to the mind, and their connection with objects cannot be experienced.

The sceptics always triumph here, arguing that, if people follow their natural instincts, they will believe they perceive external objects, but, if they treat perceptions as only representations of something external, they abandon natural instinct, and are unable to find a convincing argument connecting perceptions with external objects. Further, it is generally accepted that such sensible qualities as hard, soft and hot do not exist in the objects, but are secondary perceptions of the mind, so this must also apply to the supposed primary qualities of extension and solidity, which are acquired from the senses of sight and feeling. However, an extension that is neither tangible nor visible is inconceivable. Thus, if belief in external existence of objects is based on the evidence of the senses and natural instinct, it is contrary to reason, but if it is referred to reason, it is contrary to natural instinct. Further, it is against reason for primary and secondary qualities to be in objects, but if matter is stripped of them, what remains is just an unknown something, which causes perceptions.

Part 2 (pp. 204–7)

Sceptics object to both abstract reasonings and those about fact and existence. And, indeed, with the former, quite apart from what the sceptics say, our conclusions about, for example, the properties of circles and triangles do amaze reason. But scepticism provides no answers: on the contrary, nothing creates more hesitation and doubt than scepticism itself. Sceptical objections to reasoning about matters of fact are either popular or philosophical. The former, which arise from the limitations of human understanding, and the fact that people hold different opinions about things, are weak. Action and everyday activity are the best ways to drive out sceptical views of this kind. They may flourish in the university or study, where it seems impossible to refute them, but they disappear in the outside world, where even the most determined sceptic is unable to sustain them.

The sceptic is on firmer ground with philosophical objections. He can argue that, apart from sense and memory, our only evidence for any matter of fact is the relation of cause and effect; that this derives from observing the constant conjunction of two objects; that we have no basis, apart from custom or instinct, for believing they will continue to be; and that these may deceive us. The most powerful objection to excessive scepticism is that it does no lasting good and is of no benefit to society. Human life would perish, if such views prevailed, as people would sink into total inactivity. But nature is too strong. The extreme sceptic may astound himself or others, for a time, but the most trivial event will expel his doubts, leaving him in the same state as everyone else. He will have to admit that his objections merely highlight the whimsical nature of human beings, who act and reason and believe, even though they cannot satisfy themselves about the basis of their beliefs.

Part 3 (pp. 207–11)

Human beings tend to be dogmatic in their opinions, and to see only one side of an argument, so limited scepticism brings out the limitations of human understanding, makes people more receptive to the views of others, and leads even educated people to realize that what they know is insignificant, compared to the complexity and confusion, inherent in human nature. It might also convince us to confine our enquiries to subjects, suited to the narrow limits of human understanding. The imagination may soar to the extraordinary, but human beings should concentrate on matters relating to ordinary life and experience, where many things need to be corrected and put in order. There is no explanation of why a stone falls, or fire burns, so we are unlikely to reach satisfactory conclusions about the origin of worlds.

Examination of the powers of the human mind shows how appropriate this approach is. The existence of any being can only be proved by arguing from its cause or effect; it is only experience that enables us to infer the existence of one object from another; and this is the source of most human knowledge and action. History and geography are about particular facts, the sciences and politics about general ones. Theology comprises both, and, as it is supported by experience, has a basis in reason. However, its real foundation is faith and divine revelation. Morals and criticism are matters of taste, rather than understanding. Applying these principles would cause havoc in a library. It would be asked, of a book about divinity or metaphysics, whether it contained any abstract reasoning about quantity or number, or any experimental reasoning about matters of fact or existence. If it did not, it could be committed to the flames as sophistry and illusion.

Glossary

Abbé Paris, the famous Jansenist. François de Paris (1690–1727), a follower of Bishop Cornelius Jansen (see Jansenism below). Miracles were said to take place at his tomb.

Absolute contradiction/contradiction. Bringing together a proposition and its negation.

Abstract sciences. Science, the sciences.

Abstraction. Getting the ideas of the primary qualities of extension and solidity by identifying, and then abstracting them, as common features of a number of objects.

Abstruse/abstract philosophy. Philosophy, as opposed to moralizing or guidance about right conduct. See philosophy below.

Academical philosophy. Limited and constructive scepticism, as opposed to Pyrrhonism.

Achilles. In Homer's *Iliad*, the principal hero on the Greek side during the Trojan War.

Addison, Joseph (1672–1719). Essayist, poet and playwright and Whig politician, who was co-founder of *The Spectator*.

Adjust its parts. Some people claim that God is the cause of everything that happens in the world. Hume suggests it would reflect less well on God and his power, if he had made a world, which, instead of operating according to predictable laws of nature, and which provides a stable environment, required him to intervene continually in its operation, in order to put it right.

Aenid. Virgil's (Publius Vergilius Maro, 70–19 BC) 12-book epic poem about the adventures of Aeneas, the legendary founder of the Roman state, after the fall of Troy.

Age and country. Ancient Greece and Athens.

Alexander. A false prophet, who claimed that Asclepius, the god of healing, was born from a goose egg.

Almighty (the). God.

Glossary

Analogy. Drawing a parallel between two things on the basis of similarities between them.

Antecedent scepticism. Scepticism, such as that of Descartes in his *Meditations on First Philosophy*, which comes before philosophical investigation, and is the basis on which it is conducted; universal doubt which doubts everything.

Apology. Vindication, defence of.

Apostles (the). Messengers: in particular, Jesus' 12 disciples, who were sent to preach the gospel.

A priori. That which comes before, and is known independently of experience, and which holds (or is claimed to hold) irrespective of experience, such as mathematical truths.

Aristotle (384–322 BC). Greek philosopher, student of Plato and author of such books as the *De Interpretatione*, *The Nicomachean Ethics* and *Metaphysics*.

Atheist. One who is convinced there is no God, as opposed to an agnostic, who merely doubts God's existence.

Athens. City-state in ancient Greece, which played a major part in defeating the Persian invasions of Greece, established a democratic system of government, and was famous as a seat of learning. The philosophers, Socrates and Plato were Athenians, and Aristotle studied there at Plato's Academy.

Attributes (of God). God's characteristics, such as (in Christianity) his (infinite) power, goodness and mercy.

Auditors. Listeners.

Augmenting. Adding to.

Avarice. Greed.

Bacon, Francis, Viscount St Albans (1561–1626). English philosopher, scientist, lawyer, statesman, who was Lord Chancellor during the reign of James I. His books include *The Advancement of Learning*, *Novum Organum* and *Essays*.

Belief. To hold that something (such as a proposition) is true. Hume maintains (Section 5) that the feeling or sentiment, attached to belief, constitutes the only difference between a proposition about a matter of fact or existence we accept and one we reject.

Benevolence. Desire to do good. In Christianity (infinite) benevolence is believed to be an attribute of God, who wishes human beings (his creatures) well.

Caesar. Any Roman emperor.

Canons. Clergy who are members of a cathedral chapter, or church laws.

Glossary

Cardinal de Retz (1613–79). An archbishop of Paris.

Cartesian doubt. The kind of doubt Descartes describes in his *Meditations on First Philosophy*: extreme and comprehensive doubt of everything he previously believed, in order to discover what is certain.

Causation. Causal relationships, the relation between two objects or events, such that when one is present, or occurs, it produces, or leads to, the other.

Cause. That which brings about a certain effect.

Centaur. A horse that has a human body, arms and head.

Chance. That which happens without design or intention.

Cicero, Marcus Tullus (106–43 BC). Roman statesman, lawyer and orator, whose books include *On Duty, On the Republic* and *On the Nature of the Gods*.

Collateral. Parallel, subordinate but from the same source.

Complex. Having many parts.

Compounding. Here, combining, putting together.

Consequent scepticism. Scepticism arising from philosophical or scientific investigation, which Hume discusses in Section 12.

Constraint. Compulsion. Hume maintains (Section 8) that human beings are free, unless they are subject to external constraint.

Contiguity in time or place. Proximity in time or place.

Contradictory phaenomenon. Thing that appears to be at odds with (something else).

Controul events, and govern futurity. Control events and determine what happens in the future.

Correlative. That which corresponds to, has a mutual relationship with.

Correspondent idea. The idea that corresponds to (the particular sensation).

Court of judicature. Court concerned with the administration of justice.

Creator. God.

Deity (the). God.

Demonstrative reasoning. Reasoning related to *a priori* (see above) knowledge.

Demonstratively certain. That which is absolutely certain, such that its denial would involve a contradiction.

Descartes, René (1596–1650). French rationalist philosopher, and author of *Meditations on First Philosophy, Discourse on Method* and *The Principles of Philosophy*. See also Cartesian doubt above.

Design (argument). One of the traditional arguments for the existence of God, which points to similarities between the world and objects designed and made by human beings, and argues that, as the effects are similar, so must be the causes. Hume develops his criticism of the argument in detail in his *Dialogues Concerning Natural Religion*.

Determinate. Definite, distinct.

Determinism. The doctrine that every event has a cause. Applied to what are held to be voluntary human actions, it suggests they are not actually free. There are three main philosophical responses to this issue: 'soft determinism' (the position adopted by Hume in Section 8), which argues that human freedom is compatible with determinism, and that human beings are free, unless subject to external constraint; 'hard determinism', which holds that the causal connection between human motives and actions rules out genuine human freedom; and libertarianism, which maintains that the human will is free, and must be so if human beings are to be held responsible for their actions.

Divinity. In the *Enquiry*, either God or a book about God/religious matters.

Doctrine of necessity. That, in the universe, laws of nature determine exactly what is going to happen, such that nature operates uniformly and predictably, creating a stable environment (Section 8).

Dogma. (Religious) belief accepted on authority, and which may be held despite there being a lack of supporting evidence or even evidence that it is not true.

Dogmatical. Insisting something is true, despite inadequate or contrary evidence.

Dye. Old term for dice.

Easy philosophy. That which is concerned only with inculcating moral principles and ensuring right conduct.

Effect. What results from a cause, its consequence(s).

Empirical/empiricist. That which relates to, or is based on, experience. Empiricists maintain that experience is human beings' only source of knowledge of the world.

Epic poetry. Long poems, which narrate the deeds of a hero(es), as in Homer's *Iliad* and *Odyssey*.

Epicurus (341–270 BC). Greek philosopher who settled and taught in Athens. He held that knowledge comes through the senses; that superstition should be eliminated; and that pleasure (as the only one known to the senses) is the sole good.

Epicurean. Follower of Epicurus.

Glossary

Epistemology. Theory of knowledge, theories about what human beings know, how they know what they (claim to) know and the limits of human knowledge.

Established superstition. The prevailing religious beliefs.

Evil and disorder. Features of the world that suggest it was not made by an (all-) powerful and (all-) benevolent God. Critics of the design argument (see above) ask why, if God designed the world, he did not make it a better place (one without evil and disorder).

Exigence of human life. Emergency or urgent need that arises in life.

Experience (and observation). What relates to the empirical world, and the way human beings experience things, which some people (empiricists) consider to be the only source of knowledge of the world.

Experience of his productions, in the usual course of nature. All that we know about God and his attributes comes from what we can learn from the ordinary operations of nature/the universe (assuming that we believe it was created by God).

Extension (physical). That physical things are extended and occupy space.

Extension and solidity. See primary qualities below.

External universe/world/objects. The universe and the things it contains, which exist independently of us, and about which our senses give us information.

Faculty. Power, power of the mind.

Faith. In a religious context, either simply religious belief/belief in God or trusting belief in God, which is not supported by clear evidence.

Forged miracles. False miracles.

General laws. Laws of nature, which make the universe a stable and predictable environment.

Grecian. Greek.

Hard determinism. See determinism above.

Hector. Son of Priam, King of Troy, and leader of the Trojan forces, who was killed by Achilles during the siege of Troy.

Helen. Beautiful wife of Menelaus, King of Sparta, whose elopement with Paris, son of Priam, King of Troy, led to the Trojan War.

Holy Spirit. In Christian theology, one of the three persons of the Trinity (God is three in one: Father, Son and Holy Spirit), who is the inspirer and sustainer of Christians and the Christian Church.

Human soul. Hume uses the terms 'mind' and 'soul' interchangeably. The issue is the difficult one of how mind/soul and body are related.

Glossary

Hypothesis. A theory put forward as a basis for reasoning, or starting-point for discussion.

Idea(s). Thought or recollection of, for example, objects or emotions, as opposed to the direct perception or sensation of them.

Image. Representation of something: what is present to the mind is not an external object, but an image or perception of it (Section 12).

Image(s) (religious). Statue or picture of saint or holy person.

Imagination. The human ability to form images or pictures in the mind.

Impression(s). The direct perception or sensation of objects or emotions.

Indifference and contingency of human actions. That human actions are unpredictable, and do not seem to have been predetermined by God.

Inference/infer. Concluding one thing from something else.

Infinite divisibility. Capable of being divided an infinite number of times.

Infinitely intelligent, wise, and good Being. God, whose characteristics are thought to be (according to Christian teaching) infinite or unlimited.

Intelligent cause. God, as the cause of the universe.

Intuitive/intuition. Immediate mental awareness/apprehension (of something).

Inveterate revenge. Long-established, deep-rooted (desire for) revenge.

Invisible intelligent principle. An unseen, supernatural cause.

Jansenism. A reform movement within the Roman Catholic Church, founded by Cornelius Jansen (1585–1638, Bishop of Ypres), which taught absolute predestinationism (that God has preordained individuals' salvation or damnation).

Jupiter. Originally a sky-spirit, he came to be seen as the chief Roman god, and was identified with the Greek god, Zeus.

Law of motion. Isaac Newton's three laws of motion, which explain how objects move and how they respond to forces.

Libertarianism. See determinism above.

Liberty. Freedom. In Section 8, Hume defines it as: the power of acting, or not acting, according to the determinations of the will. In this section, he is concerned with the questions of what is meant by human actions being free, and the extent to which they are free.

Locke, John (1632–1704). British empiricist philosopher, medical practitioner and administrator, whose books include *Essay Con-*

cerning Human Understanding, Two Treatises of Government and *The Reasonableness of Christianity*.

Lodestone. An oxide of iron that attracts metal objects.

Lucian (Lucianus, c. AD 155–c. 200). Rhetorician and writer from Samosata (in modern Turkey), who wrote satiric dialogues, such as *Dialogues of the Gods* and *Dialogues of the Dead*, directed at religious superstitions and myths.

Marcus Aurelius (AD 121–80). Roman emperor from 161 to 180, he spent most of his reign fighting Rome's enemies. He wrote his *Meditations* during his campaigns.

Matters of fact. Empirical things, those known through experience.

Maxim. Rule or principle.

Mediate cause. Indirect cause.

Mental geography. Nature of the human mind.

Metaphysical jargon. Specialized terms, used in metaphysics, which may be hard for non-specialists to understand.

Metaphysics. Study of what is after (beyond) physics, and which cannot be investigated by ordinary empirical methods; the investigation of what really exists, of ultimate reality.

Milton, John (1608–74). English poet and supporter of the parliamentary cause, during and after the English Civil War, whose works include *Paradise Lost, Paradise Regained* and the *Areopagitica* (calling for freedom of the press).

Miracle. An event that cannot be accounted for according to established laws of nature, which it appears to break, and which is attributed to God/supernatural causes.

Mixed mathematics. The use of geometry to aid scientific investigation.

Moral ill(s). Moral evil(s): human actions that cause suffering, such as violence, torture and theft.

Moral philosophy. A term used by Hume in a broader sense than it is today, to refer to the human mind and human motivation, as well as moral issues and the general principles of morality.

Moral sciences. Studies concerned with human beings and human conduct. Moral science is an old term for philosophy.

Moralists. Those who enquire into, teach or practise morality.

Natural philosophy. Natural science(s).

Necessary connexion. Two objects or events being linked necessarily, such that the occurrence of one is always followed by occurrence of the other.

Necessity. That which must occur.

Glossary

Odyssey. Homer's epic poem, which describes the adventures of Odysseus, King of Ithaca, as he returns home from Troy.

Omen. Event or object that gives warning that something good or evil will happen.

Omniscience. All-knowing. According to Christian teaching, God's knowledge is infinite, so he is all-knowing.

Oracle. Prophecy, or person making prophecy.

Ovid (Publius Ovidius Naso, 43 BC–AD 18). Roman poet, exiled from Rome by the Emperor Augustus, whose works include *Ars Amatoria*, the *Metamorphoses* and the *Tristia*.

Pamphlagonians. Inhabitants of Pamphlagonia in Asia Minor (modern Turkey).

Paradise Lost. Milton's poem, which tells the story of the fall of Adam.

Passage to something farther. Life after death: seeing this life as a preparation for the next.

Peloponnesian War. War between Athens and Sparta for supremacy in Greece, which ended with the defeat of Athens in 404 BC.

Perceptions of the mind/perceptions. What is immediately seen, heard or felt. See also impression(s) above.

Philosopher. One who studies and practises/teaches philosophy.

Philosophy. Literally, love of wisdom. The study of ultimate reality, what really exists, the most general principles of things.

Physical ill(s). Natural evil(s): natural features of the world that cause suffering, such as diseases, hurricanes and floods.

Popular superstitions. Widely held and irrational beliefs or fears.

Power of acting, or not acting, according to the determinations of the will. Being able to act or not act as the will determines: thus, to be free of external compulsion.

Precept(s). Maxim or rule.

Preordained and predetermined. Laid down and ordered beforehand (by God).

Prescience. Foreknowledge. It is argued that, if God knows what is going to happen, before it occurs, there can be no such thing as human freedom.

Priestly dogmas. Dogmas (see above) associated with clergy or a church.

Primary qualities. The fundamental properties (extension and solidity) of things, which, unlike the secondary qualities, such as smell and colour, are not perceived by one sense only.

Principles of association. The principles that connect ideas. Hume

Glossary

holds that there are three: resemblance, contiguity in time or place and cause and effect (Section 3).

Principle of connexion. See principles of association above.

Principle of custom or habit. Hume argues that it is through observing the constant conjunction of certain objects or events, that we infer the existence of one from the appearance of the other, even though we do not know how one produces the other.

Probability. One event or outcome being more likely to occur than another.

Prodigies. Marvellous events, which cannot be explained according to established laws of nature.

Proposition. Statement, which may or may not be true.

Protagoras (born c. 485 BC). Greek philosopher and sophist, who was expelled from Athens for his atheist views.

Providence. God's beneficent care and ordering of his creation.

Pyrrhonism. Method of doubt associated with the Greek philosopher, Pyrrho of Elis (c. 365–275 BC), who established a profoundly sceptical approach to philosophical enquiry.

Queen Elizabeth. Queen Elizabeth I (1533–1603). She succeeded her half-sister, Mary, as Queen of England in 1558, and was succeeded by her cousin, James I (James VI of Scotland) in 1603.

Ratiocination. Going through logical processes, formal reasoning.

Rationalist. A philosopher (such as Descartes), who believes that reason, rather than (sense) experience is the (principal) source of human knowledge.

Real presence. The belief that Christ's body and blood are actually present in the bread and wine at the Eucharist (holy communion).

Reasoning concerning matter of fact and existence. Reasoning about matters known through experience/the senses, as distinct from demonstrative reasoning (see above).

Relations of ideas. Propositions concerning *a priori* knowledge, as in mathematics and logic, denial of which involves a contradiction.

Relict(s). Bodily part of, or something that belonged to, a saint or holy person.

Religionist. A religious person, member of a particular religious faith.

Religious tradition of your forefathers. The traditional religious beliefs of the Athenians: in the Greek gods.

Revealed/revelation. What God chooses to disclose of himself to human beings through, for example, holy scriptures and prophets.

Roman Catholic ceremonies. The rituals of the Roman Catholic

Glossary

Church. Hume uses them (Section 5) to illustrate the role of resemblance as a principle of association.

Saragossa. City in Spain.

Sceptic/scepticism. Generally, doubt, or refusing to accept non-empirical sources of knowledge. See also Pyrrhonism and Cartesian doubt above.

Science of human nature. See moral philosophy above.

Secondary qualities. The qualities of objects, such as colour and smell, that are immediately perceived by the senses.

Sensation. See idea(s) and impression(s) above.

Sensible qualities. Qualities that are known through the senses.

Sentiments. Feelings, views.

Siam. Old name for Thailand.

Siege of Athens. This took place at the end of the Peloponnesian War, and led to the final defeat of Athens by Sparta.

Simple. That which has only one element or part.

Sin. Offence against God, act that breaks God's law.

Socrates (c. 470–399 BC). Greek philosopher, who features in the works of Plato, and devoted his life to the pursuit of philosophical truth. He was executed by the Athenians for undermining belief in the gods and corrupting their youth.

Soft determinism. See determinism above.

Sophistry. Quibbling, misleading reasoning. In ancient Greece, the sophists were teachers of rhetoric, who attached more importance to the way things were expressed than their substance.

Stoic. School of Greek philosophy, which taught self-control and uncomplaining fortitude in the face of pain and adversity.

Sublime. Awe-inspiring, uplifting.

Supernatural. That which is above or beyond nature, and which cannot be explained according to physical laws.

Superstitious delusion. False opinion, based on irrational belief about the supernatural.

Supreme being. God.

That philosopher. The physicist and mathematician, Sir Isaac Newton (1642–1727), whose scientific laws explained the movements of bodies in the universe.

Theology. Setting out the beliefs and teachings of a religion in a systematic way; academic discipline concerned with the study of religion/religious beliefs.

Tillotson, John (1630–94). Anglican theologian and Archbishop of Canterbury.

Glossary

Transposing. Changing the order or position of things.

Ultimate cause of any natural operation. What is ultimately responsible for any event in nature/the universe.

Unity of action. The unity of action found in literary works of any kind, as they describe how one action depends on another.

Universal law. Law of nature, which applies invariably.

Unknown spirit. In his *Meditations on First Philosophy*, Descartes imagines that a wicked and all-powerful being is using all its skill to deceive him.

Venus. Roman goddess identified with Aphrodite, the Greek goddess of love and beauty.

Veracity of the supreme being. In his *Meditations on First Philosophy*, Descartes concludes that God does not send sense experiences himself, or via another creature, and as he has strongly inclined human beings to believe that they come from external objects, they must do so.

Virtue. Generally, moral excellence, a positive character trait that makes someone morally good and admirable.

Volition. Act of willing

Vulgar (the). Ordinary, uneducated people.

Will (the). The capability of wishing for something and using one's mental powers to try to accomplish it.